Erased In A Moment:

Suicide Bombing Attacks Against Israeli Civilians

Human Rights Watch
New York • Washington • London • Brussels

ISBN: 1-56432-280-7
Library of Congress Control Number: 2002114404

Cover photos:
Relatives and friends mourn during a funeral for victims of a March 9,
2002, suicide bombing attack at the Cafe Moment in Jerusalem. Eleven
civilians were killed and more than fifty were injured in the attack.
Hamas claimed responsibility. (c) 2002 Reuters Ltd.

An Israeli civilian injured in the May 19, 2002, suicide bombing attack
at the Netanya market receives help. Three civilians were killed and
more than thirty were injured. The attack was claimed by Hamas and the
Popular Front for the Liberation of Palestine. (c) 2002 Reuters Ltd.

Cover design by Rafael Jiménez

Addresses for Human Rights Watch
350 Fifth Avenue, 34th Floor, New York, NY 10118-3299
Tel: (212) 290-4700, Fax: (212) 736-1300, E-mail: hrwnyc@hrw.org

1630 Connecticut Avenue, N.W., Suite 500, Washington, DC 20009
Tel: (202) 612-4321, Fax: (202) 612-4333, E-mail: hrwdc@hrw.org

2nd Floor, 2-12 Pentonville Road London N1 9HF, UK
Tel: (44 20) 7713 1995, Fax: (44 20) 7713 1800, E-mail: hrwuk@hrw.org

15 Rue Van Campenhout, 1000 Brussels, Belgium
Tel: (32 2) 732-2009, Fax: (32 2) 732-0471, E-mail: hrwbe@hrw.org

Web Site Address: http://www.hrw.org
Web Site Address in Arabic: http//www.hrrw.org/arabic

Listserv address: To subscribe to the list, send an e-mail message to
hrw-news-subscribe@igc.topica.com with "subscribe hrw-news" in the body of
the message (leave the subject line blank).

Human Rights Watch is dedicated to
protecting the human rights of people around the world.

We stand with victims and activists to prevent
discrimination, to uphold political freedom, to protect people from inhumane
conduct in wartime, and to bring offenders to justice.

We investigate and expose
human rights violations and hold abusers accountable.

We challenge governments and those who hold power to end abusive practices
and respect international human rights law.

We enlist the public and the international
community to support the cause of human rights for all.

HUMAN RIGHTS WATCH

Human Rights Watch conducts regular, systematic investigations of human rights abuses in some seventy countries around the world. Our reputation for timely, reliable disclosures has made us an essential source of information for those concerned with human rights. We address the human rights practices of governments of all political stripes, of all geopolitical alignments, and of all ethnic and religious persuasions. Human Rights Watch defends freedom of thought and expression, due process and equal protection of the law, and a vigorous civil society; we document and denounce murders, disappearances, torture, arbitrary imprisonment, discrimination, and other abuses of internationally recognized human rights. Our goal is to hold governments accountable if they transgress the rights of their people.

Human Rights Watch began in 1978 with the founding of its Europe and Central Asia division (then known as Helsinki Watch). Today, it also includes divisions covering Africa, the Americas, Asia, and the Middle East. In addition, it includes three thematic divisions on arms, children's rights, and women's rights. It maintains offices in New York, Washington, Los Angeles, London, Brussels, Moscow, Tashkent, Tblisi, and Bangkok. Human Rights Watch is an independent, nongovernmental organization, supported by contributions from private individuals and foundations worldwide. It accepts no government funds, directly or indirectly.

The staff includes Kenneth Roth, executive director; Michele Alexander, development and outreach director; Rory Mungoven, advocacy director; Carroll Bogert, communications director; John T. Green, operations director, Barbara Guglielmo, finance and administration director; Lotte Leicht, Brussels office director; Patrick Minges, publications director; Maria Pignataro Nielsen, human resources director; Joe Saunders, interim program director; Wilder Tayler, legal and policy director; and Joanna Weschler, United Nations representative. Jonathan Fanton is the chair of the board. Robert L. Bernstein is the founding chair.

The regional division directors of Human Rights Watch are Peter Takirambudde, Africa; José Miguel Vivanco, Americas; Brad Adams, Asia; Elizabeth Andersen, Europe and Central Asia; and Hanny Megally, Middle East and North Africa. The thematic division directors are Steve Goose, Arms (acting); Lois Whitman, Children's Rights; and LaShawn R. Jefferson, Women's Rights.

The members of the board of directors are Jonathan Fanton, Chair; Robert L. Bernstein, Founding Chair, Khaled Abou El Fadl, Lisa Anderson, Lloyd Axworthy, David Brown, William Carmichael, Dorothy Cullman, Irene Diamond, Edith Everett, Michael Gellert, Vartan Gregorian, Alice H. Henkin, James F. Hoge, Jr., Stephen L. Kass, Marina Pinto Kaufman, Wendy Keys, Bruce Klatsky, Joanne Leedom-Ackerman, Josh Mailman, Joel Motley, Samuel K. Murumba, Jane Olson, Peter Osnos, Kathleen Peratis, Catherine Powell, Bruce Rabb, Sigrid Rausing, Orville Schell, Sid Sheinberg, Gary G. Sick, Domna Stanton, John J. Studzinski, Shibley Telhami, Maureen White, and Maya Wiley. Emeritus Board: Roland Algrant, Adrian DeWind, and Malcolm Smith.

ACKNOWLEDGEMENTS

This report was researched and written by Joe Stork, Washington director of the Middle East and North Africa division of Human Rights Watch. Miranda Sissons, researcher for the Middle East and North Africa division and Johanna Bjorken, a consultant, assisted in research and writing. Jessica Bonn, a consultant, conducted additional interviews. Hanny Megally, executive director of the Middle East and North Africa division, edited the report. Wilder Tayler, the legal and policy director, provided legal review. Research assistance was provided by Dalia Haj Omar and James Darrow, associates with the Middle East and North Africa division; Tahirih Sariban and Juan Valdivieso, interns; and Na'ameh Razon, a 2002 Everett Fellow. Dalia Haj Omar and Mohamed Abdel Dayem, an associate with the Middle East and North Africa division, assisted with Arabic translation. The report was prepared for publication by Jonathan Horowitz, program coordinator; Leila Hull, associate with the Middle East and North Africa division; Patrick Minges of the communications division, and Jessica Thorpe, a consultant.

Human Rights Watch also thanks the many individuals who agreed to speak with us in the course of this research, as well as others who provided assistance in interpreting, locating information referred to in the report, but who wished not to be acknowledged by name.

Human Rights Watch acknowledges the support of NOVIB, the Dutch Organization for International Development Cooperation, Member of Eurostep and Oxfam International, for its research in Israel, the Occupied West Bank and Gaza Strip, and Palestinian Authority Territories.

ABOUT THIS REPORT

This report is based on field research, expert and witness interviews, and examination of public documents. Field research was carried out during two Human Rights Watch investigative missions to Israel, the West Bank, and the Gaza Strip in May-June 2002. During these visits, Human Rights Watch interviewed members of armed groups, victims, families of perpetrators, PA officials, current and former PA security officers, Israeli and Palestinian analysts and security experts, diplomats and other foreign officials, and Palestinian activists and militants.

Documents consulted included those that Israel says were seized by the Israel Defense Forces (IDF) from Palestinian Authority offices in April-May 2002 and at other times, and made public on the websites of the IDF and the Israeli Ministry of Foreign Affairs, along with extensive commentary by official Israeli analysts. In addition, Human Rights Watch asked Israeli government officials to provide any additional evidence or documentation to support the government's charges concerning Palestinian Authority complicity in suicide bombings against civilians. The information provided by the government in response to this request largely reproduced information already available.

Human Rights Watch has assumed the authenticity of these documents, although we note that PA officials have dismissed the released documents in general terms as fabrications. Where Human Rights Watch has used these documents, it has done so based upon its own analysis and translation. Human Rights Watch notes that the documents have been released selectively, over time, and in various configurations, hampering any rigorous assessment of the significance and sequence of incidents described in them. Human Rights Watch also notes that the IDF official analysis and commentary concerning the documents made available frequently appears to be based on additional materials that, though mentioned in the IDF analysis and commentary, were themselves not publicly accessible at the time of writing.

Table of Contents

I. SUMMARY

More than 415 Israeli and other civilians have been killed, and more than two thousand injured, as a result of attacks by armed Palestinians between September 30, 2000 and August 31, 2002. The majority of these deaths and injuries were caused by so-called suicide bombings carried out by Palestinians. Typically, the bombers, who surrendered their own lives in the process, sought to set off their explosions in places where civilians were gathered, including restaurants and places of entertainment—"soft" targets where they could expect to cause the largest number of casualties. Typically, too, the bombers packed the explosives with nails and pieces of metal for extra deadly effect. In addition to the toll of deaths and injuries, the bombings have sown widespread fear among the civilian population—as they were intended to do.

Hamas and Islamic Jihad, two Islamist Palestinian groups, had previously carried out suicide bombings against Israeli targets in the mid-1990s, as part of their opposition to the Oslo Accords and, at times, the Palestinian Authority (PA). At that time the PA clamped down, arresting some 1,200 leaders and activists, and the bombings ceased. Some of those detained were held for long periods without charge or trial. The PA freed those who remained in detention soon after the current uprising—widely known as the al-Aqsa Intifada—began in September 2000. Within months, following a rapid escalation of violence on both sides, Hamas again resorted to suicide bombings against Israeli civilians when, on January 1, 2001, a suicide bomber blew himself up at a crowded bus station in Netanya, wounding at least twenty civilians. Islamic Jihad resumed suicide attacks against civilians shortly afterwards.

Throughout 2001, there was a rash of such attacks, peaking in March, November, and early December. Israel charged that President Yasir Arafat and the PA were responsible because they had failed to rein in the Islamist groups. In June and again in December 2001, in response to mounting international pressure, the PA obtained a cessation of suicide bombings (though not all attacks) against civilians. These lasted for some six weeks beginning in early June and for some four weeks beginning in mid-December. On January 14, 2002, Israeli forces killed a local West Bank leader of the al-Aqsa Martyrs' Brigades (the al-Aqsa Brigades), which had been formed at the start of the current clashes and is affiliated with Arafat's Fatah organization. The al-Aqsa Brigades carried out their first suicide bombing two weeks later—the first to be carried out by a female perpetrator. The blast killed one civilian and injured one hundred. A fourth group, the Popular Front for the Liberation of Palestine (PFLP), also carried out suicide bombings in 2002.

Each of these four groups has attacked civilians repeatedly. The scale and systematic nature of these attacks in 2001 and 2002 meet the definition of a crime against humanity. When these suicide bombings take place in the context of violence that amounts to armed conflict, they are also war crimes. Human Rights Watch unreservedly condemns these atrocities.

Of the four groups, three have an adversarial relationship with Arafat and the PA: Hamas, Islamic Jihad, and the PFLP. The fourth, the al-Aqsa Martyrs' Brigades, proclaims its support for Arafat and the PA. Inevitably, the attacks carried out by the al-Aqsa Brigades have provoked the most questions, with intense speculation as to whether they were sanctioned by, or carried out at the behest of, Arafat. This report examines that question, among others.

The Palestinian Authority is not a state, and is therefore not a party to the major international humanitarian law treaties, but it has on several occasions signaled its willingness to abide by those standards. International humanitarian law, through the well established doctrine of command responsibility, requires that those who occupy positions of authority cannot escape accountability for war crimes or other grave abuses committed by persons under their control if they ordered their subordinates to commit such crimes, failed to take reasonable preventive action, or failed to punish the perpetrators. This doctrine is particularly relevant to those in the military chain of command, but the doctrine also extends to political and other leaders insofar as they have "effective responsibility and control" over the actors in question.[1] The leaders of Hamas and Islamic Jihad, in particular, appear to be criminal offenders under that doctrine: many of them have openly espoused, encouraged, or endorsed suicide bombing attacks against Israeli civilians, and appear to have had the capacity to turn the bombings on and off at will. The PFLP, which has claimed responsibility for car bombings as well as several suicide bombings that targeted civilians, appears to have a similar degree of internal cohesion and centralized authority, thus making its leadership also criminally liable.

Human Rights Watch sought particularly to obtain information that would enable it to assess the role and responsibility of the PA, as the entity charged with maintaining security in select areas of the West Bank and Gaza Strip. Our conclusion, on the basis of the available public information, is that there are important steps that Arafat and the PA could and should have taken to prevent or deter suicide bombings directed against civilians. The failure to take those steps implies a high degree of responsibility for what occurred. Individual members of the al-Aqsa Brigades have even been among the beneficiaries of payments

---

[1] Rome Statute of the International Criminal Court, Article 28(b), U.N. Doc. no. A/CONF. 183/9 (July 17, 1998), 37 I.L.M. 999.

approved by Arafat personally at a time when he knew or should have known that such individuals were alleged to have been involved in planning or carrying out attacks on civilians.

The greatest failure of President Arafat and the PA leadership—a failure for which they must bear heavy responsibility—is their unwillingness to deploy the criminal justice system decisively to stop the suicide bombings, particularly in 2001, when the PA was most capable of doing so. President Arafat and the PA also failed to take aggressive measures to ensure that the intensely polarized political atmosphere not serve as a justification for such attacks. Certain Israeli actions, such as the destruction of PA police and security installations, gradually undermined the PA's capacity to act. But even when their capacity to act was largely intact, Arafat and the PA took no effective action to bring to justice those in Hamas, Islamic Jihad, the PFLP, and the al-Aqsa Martyrs' Brigades who incited, planned or assisted in carrying out bombings and other attacks on Israeli civilians. Instead, Arafat and the PA pursued a policy whereby suspects, when they were detained, were not investigated or prosecuted, but typically were soon let out onto the street again. Indeed, the PA leadership appeared to treat its duty to prosecute murderers as something that was negotiable and contingent on Israel's compliance with its undertakings in the Oslo Accords, not as the unconditional obligation that it was.

The PA sought to explain these releases by citing the danger to detainees when Israeli forces bombed places of detention. But the PA has not explained why suspects were never investigated, charged, or tried — steps that could have been taken with little or no risk to the suspects' physical well-being. Further, while Arafat has repeatedly and publicly condemned suicide bombings and other attacks against Israeli civilians, he has done little to confront or correct the positive portrayal of the bombers within the Palestinian community as "martyrs." Indeed, several PA officials have praised attacks on civilians. Again, steps to delegitimize attacks on civilians could have been taken despite Israel's degradation of the PA's administrative and security apparatus. Finally, Arafat and the PA failed to take available administrative steps to ensure that there were no financial incentives for carrying out attacks on civilians. In a handful of cases, President Arafat authorized modest payments to people whom he knew or should have known had attacked civilians. More commonly, President Arafat and the PA did not take adequate steps as the established authority in the area to prevent special payments, by the PA or others, to such perpetrators and their families. This inaction fostered an environment that allowed Palestinian armed groups to believe they could attack civilians with impunity.

On the basis of what was publicly available as of the end of September 2002, Human Rights Watch did not find evidence that Arafat and the PA planned, ordered, or carried out suicide bombings or other attacks on Israeli civilians. Despite the links between President Arafat's Fatah organization and the al-Aqsa Martyrs' Brigades, we found no evidence that the al-Aqsa Brigades, when planning or carrying out suicide bombings or other attacks on civilians, took their orders from or sought the endorsement of Arafat or other senior PA or Fatah leaders. Rather, the al-Aqsa Brigades appear to operate with a wide degree of local discretion and to maintain only a loose relationship with Arafat and the senior Fatah leadership. Such a relationship does not meet the criteria required to establish that Arafat and top PA officials have command responsibility—that is, criminal liability—for the attacks against civilians carried out by the al-Aqsa Brigades. Similarly, the PA's failure to exercise its administrative and criminal justice powers to rein in independent actors does not establish command responsibility under the current state of international law. However, the lack of command responsibility in no way diminishes Arafat's and the PA's significant political responsibility for the repeated deliberate killing of civilians.

Palestinian armed groups have sought to justify suicide bombing attacks on civilians by pointing to Israeli military actions that have killed numerous Palestinian civilians during current clashes, as well as the continuing Israeli occupation of the West Bank and much of the Gaza Strip. Such excuses are completely without merit. International humanitarian law leaves absolutely no doubt that attacks targeting civilians constitute war crimes when committed in situations of armed conflict, and cross the threshold to become crimes against humanity when conducted systematically, whether in peace or war. As the latter term denotes, these are among the worst crimes that can be committed, crimes of universal jurisdiction that the international community as a whole has an obligation to punish and prevent.

International humanitarian law governing situations of armed conflict prohibits even attacks against civilians that are said to have been carried out in reprisal for attacks against one's own civilian population. This principle is set out in both the Fourth Geneva Convention and in Additional Protocol I. Even apart from these treaties, a strong trend has developed in international customary law over the past two decades to prohibit reprisals against civilians. This ban on reprisals is not dependent on reciprocal compliance by opposing forces. Even in the face of Israeli violations of international human rights and humanitarian law, Palestinian armed groups have a duty to refrain from reprisals against civilians.

Palestinian groups have also argued that they are engaged in a "liberation war" against Israel's continuing occupation, and so are somehow exempt from the obligation to respect international humanitarian law. This claim of exemption is also false. Additional Protocol I to the Geneva Conventions, which by its terms governs wars of national self-determination, states that the "civilian population as such, as well as individual civilians, shall not be the object of attack," and that "[a]cts or threats of violence the primary purpose of which is to spread terror among the civilian population are prohibited." That is, the first treaty to recognize wars of national liberation also reaffirms the prohibition of attacks on civilians. In addition, the core principles of the Geneva Conventions and their protocols are part of international customary law, indicating that they have achieved the highest degree of international consensus regardless of treaty ratifications. These include the principle requiring attacking forces to distinguish between civilians and military objects, the principle of granting civilian immunity from deliberate attack, and the prohibition against targeting civilians. All parties to a conflict are obliged unconditionally to respect these principles.

Finally, Palestinian groups have argued that Israeli settlers in the West Bank, by virtue of their presence in an occupied territory, are not civilians, and that because many Israeli adults are members of the military reserve, they, too, are legitimate military targets. These claims also run counter to international humanitarian law. Even though Israel's policy of maintaining and expanding civilian settlements in the West Bank and Gaza Strip is illegal under international humanitarian law, a person who resides in an illegal settlement continues to be a civilian unless he or she directly participates in hostilities. Except in those circumstances of direct participation in armed conflict, these residents are entitled to full protection as civilians. Similarly, international humanitarian law leaves no doubt that reserve members of military or security forces, while not on active duty, are not combatants and thus benefit from protection as civilians.

The arguments put forward to justify or excuse suicide bombings and other Palestinian attacks on civilians are without foundation. Those who articulate them either fail to understand or have decided to ignore their obligations under international humanitarian law. There can be no doubt that such attacks are grave crimes. In most, if not all cases, they are crimes against humanity. International law defines those who perpetrate these atrocities as criminals. So are those who incite, plan, and assist them. They should be brought to justice.

In this report, Human Rights Watch examines the nature and consequences—the human toll—of the suicide bombings and other attacks on civilians, reviews the relevant international humanitarian law standards and the obligations they impose, and describes the nature, structure, and objectives of the Palestinian armed groups that have carried out these attacks. As indicated, we also examine the role of the Palestinian Authority, including President Arafat.

We include specific recommendations on the steps to be taken, without delay or equivocation, to end attacks on civilians. We call on the PA and

Palestinian armed groups to end all suicide attacks against civilians and to abide by the principles of international human rights and humanitarian law. We also urge Israel to ensure that all measures to prevent or respond to suicide or other attacks against civilians conform to international humanitarian and human rights law. We call on the respective parties' international supporters to endorse these recommendations and try to enforce them, so as to help bring an end to the attacks that have cruelly claimed civilian lives and the impunity that allows these attacks to continue.

II. RECOMMENDATIONS

To the Groups Responsible for Perpetrating Suicide Bombings and Other Attacks on Civilians

Human Rights Watch unreservedly condemns suicide bombings as war crimes and crimes against humanity. We call on those responsible to desist immediately and to renounce their use unconditionally. In particular, Human Rights Watch calls on the leaders of Hamas, Islamic Jihad, the al-Aqsa Martyrs' Brigades, and the Popular Front for the Liberation of Palestine to:

- Cease such attacks immediately and declare publicly that they will not resort to such attacks in the future under any circumstances.

- Commit publicly to respecting the basic principles of international humanitarian law, and instruct all members of their organizations to do so, in particular those principles applying to the protection of civilians during armed conflict and the duty to arrest and deliver to the authorities for prosecution anyone who fails to do so.

- Cease the recruitment or use of persons under eighteen years of age in any military activities, including activities in a support role, and communicate this policy to all supporters of the group.

To President Arafat and the Palestinian Authority

Human Rights Watch recognizes that in 2002, the Palestinian Authority's capacity to maintain law and order and conduct juridical procedures is greatly diminished. Still, many of the recommendations below can be immediately implemented while others should be acted upon as the capacity of the PA is restored. Human Rights Watch calls on President Yasir Arafat and other senior officials of the Palestinian Authority to:

- Make clear that suicide bombings and other attacks on civilians constitute grave crimes; that those who incite, plan, assist, attempt, or carry out such attacks will face criminal charges; and that the PA will take all possible measures to ensure that they are brought to justice.

- Instruct the law enforcement agencies of the PA to take all possible steps, in accordance with internationally accepted human rights norms,

7

to identify and bring to justice anyone who incites, plans, assists, or attempts to carry out suicide bombings or other attacks against civilians.

- Instruct all members of the Palestinian Authority security forces that they will be severely punished if they provide any assistance, including intelligence, logistical, or other support, to those responsible for planning, assisting, or carrying out suicide bombings or other attacks on civilians. Anyone disobeying such orders should be immediately suspended, arrested, and prosecuted in a civilian court in accordance with international fair trial standards and, if convicted, sentenced to prison terms that reflect the seriousness of their crime.

- Call on all Palestinians living in the West Bank and Gaza Strip to assist the PA in bringing to an end suicide bombings and other attacks against civilians. Such an appeal should state that even if the PA's own law enforcement capacities may be diminished, the PA remains committed to fulfilling its responsibilities to end these atrocities. The PA should also set up hotlines enabling members of the public to phone in with information about potential attacks or perpetrators.

- Utilize all available media and public information systems to communicate the above messages to Palestinians in the West Bank and Gaza, and to Palestinian Arab citizens of Israel, and to call for an immediate, unconditional, and permanent halt to all suicide bombings and other attacks against civilians. Clarify that the PA does not consider as "martyrs" persons who die in the course of carrying out attacks that deliberately or indiscriminately aim to kill or cause great suffering among civilians.

- Conduct a thorough, independent investigation to identify those persons, including members of Hamas, Islamic Jihad, the Popular Front for the Liberation of Palestine, and the al-Aqsa Martyrs' Brigades who are responsible for inciting, planning, assisting, or carrying out suicide bombings or other attacks on civilians; arrest such persons; and ensure that they are prosecuted in a civilian court in accordance with international fair trial standards and, if convicted, sentenced to prison terms that reflect the seriousness of their crime. To the extent that these crimes have been carried out by or under the auspices of these organizations, take action immediately to freeze the organization's assets in order to secure them against any future claims for compensation that may be made by or on behalf of the victims.

- Take all feasible measures to prevent the recruitment and use of persons under eighteen years of age in armed hostilities, including the adoption of legal measures to prohibit and criminalize such practices.

- Declare to the Swiss Ministry of Foreign Affairs that the PA undertakes to apply the provisions of Additional Protocol I of 1977 to the Geneva Conventions of 1949, in accordance with article 96 (3) of the Protocol.

To the Government of Israel

- Ensure that all measures to prevent or respond to suicide or other attacks against civilians conform to international humanitarian and human rights law.

- Cease targeting police posts and other installations that are part of the Palestinian criminal justice infrastructure when such attacks are solely in reprisal for Palestinian attacks on Israeli targets and do not make an effective contribution to military action.

- Ensure that any restrictions on freedom of movement are implemented only when and where necessary to prevent specific acts of violence. Provide travel permits valid for use in times of closure to judges and law enforcement authorities who are essential to the functioning of the Palestinian criminal justice system. Instruct Israeli security personnel to honor such permits at checkpoints and to facilitate the passage of people holding them.

- Publicly announce that places employed by the PA for the detention of suspects and convicted prisoners will not be the object of military attack and ensure that this policy is followed.

- Ratify Additional Protocol I of 1977 to the Geneva Conventions of 1949.

To the International Community

- All governments, publicly and through diplomatic channels, should refrain from any action that appears to encourage, support or endorse suicide bombings or other attacks against civilians, and use all possible influence with the perpetrator groups to make them cease such attacks immediately and unconditionally. In particular, regional governments should use the public information media available to them to make clear that they oppose such bombings against civilians and consider those who plan or carry them out to be criminals who should be brought to justice, not "martyrs."

- All governments providing or authorizing funding or any other assistance to groups who have claimed responsibility for suicide bombings or other attacks against civilians should cease such support immediately in the absence of a public and verifiable declaration from such groups, including Hamas, Islamic Jihad, the al-Aqsa Martyrs' Brigades, and the PFLP, that they no longer associate themselves with such crimes and that they are taking effective steps to ensure that their members cease their involvement in such activities and that those who carry out the attacks are brought to justice.

- Provide technical and material support to strengthen the investigative capacity of the Palestinian Authority's law enforcement agencies including, if necessary and appropriate, through the temporary secondment of suitably qualified police investigators to work alongside Palestinian officers and to assist them in pursuing and bringing to justice those responsible for suicide bombings or other attacks against civilians.

III. SUICIDE BOMBING ATTACKS ON CIVILIANS

Introduction

"Your whole life—erased in a moment," said Moti Mizrachi, who suffered life-threatening injuries in a March 9, 2002 attack on a Jerusalem cafe. A piece of shrapnel just missed his aorta, his left hand was almost severed, and he suffered a large head wound from shrapnel.

> One quick minute and everything is radically changed. It's like your life was erased—everything that you did until age thirty-one vanished into nothing. I used to be active, to play soccer two or three times a week, I was on teams, I danced....[2]

Now, Moti Mizrachi's hand and arm are held together with pins. His life has become one of intense, protracted pain and frequent hospital visits.

The powerful bomb, detonated at the Moment Café, in the affluent Rehavia neighborhood of Jerusalem, was packed with nails and small pieces of metal. It killed eleven civilians, and wounded more than fifty.[3]

The Moment Café bombing was one of forty-eight suicide bomb attacks against Israeli civilians carried out by armed Palestinian groups between January 1, 2001 and August 31, 2002.[4] Armed groups also carried out suicide attacks directed against Israeli military targets, but this report does not address these attacks. The forty-eight attacks on civilians constituted grave crimes, including crimes against humanity. Thirty-eight of the suicide bomb attacks on civilians were carried out in Israel, including West Jerusalem; ten were carried out in the West Bank and Gaza, including East Jerusalem.

With the onset of Israeli-Palestinian clashes in September 2000, armed attacks against Israeli civilians initially took the form of shootings along roads and in built-up areas such as the settlement of Gilo on the southern outskirts of Jerusalem. Several Palestinian suicide bomb attacks against military targets were carried out during the next three months. These include car bombings that killed four Israeli civilians and wounded scores in November 2000. Islamic Jihad took credit for the first, near the popular Mahane Yehuda market in Jerusalem, which

---

[2] Human Rights Watch interview with Moti Mizrachi, age thirty-one, Jerusalem, June 23, 2002.

[3] The bombing occurred not far from the official residence of Prime Minister Sharon, who was reportedly at his Negev ranch at the time.

[4] For a full list of suicide bombing attacks against civilians from September 30, 2000 to August 31, 2002, see Appendix One.

killed two and wounded eleven.[5] Several weeks later, on November 21, a car packed with nail-studded explosives killed two and wounded more than fifty, three seriously, in the northern Israeli town of Hadera.[6]

The first suicide bomb attack against civilians after the resumption of clashes between Palestinians and Israelis in September 2000 occurred at a bus stop in Netanya on January 1, 2001. Responsibility for the attack, which wounded twenty, was claimed by Hamas (an acronym for *harakat al-muqawama al-islamiyya*, or Islamic Resistance Movement). The frequency and intensity of suicide bomb attacks on civilians soon increased, and the tactic has been embraced by large sections of the Palestinian public, making these attacks a key feature of the current Palestinian-Israeli clashes.[7]

Four groups claimed responsibility for the forty-eight suicide bomb attacks that targeted civilians. The Islamist groups Hamas and Islamic Jihad, both opponents of Yasir Arafat and the Palestinian Authority, claimed responsibility for carrying out eighteen and twelve of the attacks, respectively. The secular Popular Front for the Liberation of Palestine, another group long critical of, and opposed to Arafat and his Fatah movement, said it carried out three. The al-Aqsa Martyrs' Brigades, which is closely allied to Fatah, claimed responsibility for thirteen of the attacks, including some of the most devastating in terms of civilian casualties. Three attacks were claimed by more than one group, and

---

[5] This attack pre-empted a planned joint announcement by Prime Minister Ehud Barak and President Yasir Arafat of a truce brokered by U.S. President Bill Clinton several weeks earlier. Phil Reeves, "Truce hangs in the balance after car bomb explodes in Jerusalem," *The Independent* (London), November 3, 2000.

[6] Dina Kraft, "Two dead, more than fifty injured, in car bomb explosion in northern Israel," Associated Press, November 21, 2000. Human Rights Watch has been unable to identify a claimant for the attack.

[7] In separate reports Human Rights Watch has documented multiple violations of international humanitarian and human rights law committed during the clashes by Israeli security forces (including the excessive use of lethal force, collective punishments, the use of human shields by IDF forces, and willful killings) and Palestinian armed groups (including attacks targeting Israeli civilians and attacks that put Palestinian civilians at risk). See Human Rights Watch, "Jenin: IDF Military Operations," *A Human Rights Watch Report*, vol. 14, no. 3 (E), May 2002; Human Rights Watch, "In A Dark Hour: the Forced Use of Civilians during IDF Arrest Operations," *A Human Rights Watch Report*, vol. 14, no. 2 (E), April 2002; Human Rights Watch, "Justice Undermined: Balancing Security and Human Rights in the Palestinian Justice System," *A Human Rights Watch Report*, vol. 13, no. 4 (E), November 2001; Human Rights Watch, *Center of the Storm: A Case Study of Human Rights Abuses in Hebron District* (New York: Human Rights Watch, 2001); and Human Rights Watch, "Investigation into the Unlawful Use of Force in the West Bank, Gaza Strip and Northern Israel October 4 Through October 11," *A Human Rights Watch Report*, vol. 12, no. 3(E), October 2000.

information is not available for two attacks. All of these groups carried out other attacks on Israeli civilians, including roadside shootings in the Occupied Territories and large-scale shooting attacks, such as that on the guests at a bat mitvah party in Hadera on January 18, 2002, in which six civilians were killed and more than thirty injured.

The pace of attacks ebbed and flowed, indicating that those responsible were able to exercise at least some degree of control. Some attacks were carried out after Israeli assassinations of prominent leaders of Palestinian political and armed groups. Others appeared to have been timed to disrupt actual or potential political negotiations internally or at the international level.

Initially, only Hamas and Islamic Jihad carried out suicide bombings; these peaked in late November/early December 2001, prior to a one-month truce observed by all factions. Beginning in mid-January 2002, the al-Aqsa Martyrs' Brigades, and in February 2002, the PFLP, also carried out suicide bombings against civilians. The involvement of the al-Aqsa Martyrs' Brigades marked a significant increase in the incidence of attacks. March 2002 was the bloodiest month to date; Palestinian suicide bomb attacks killed at least eighty Israeli civilians and wounded or maimed some 420.[8]

Prior to the outbreak of clashes in late September 2000, Palestinian public support for armed attacks against Israeli targets ranged from a low of 21 percent in March 1996 to more than 40 percent at various points in the 1997-2000 period. With the collapse of the Camp David talks in July 2000, support for militant actions increased.[9] A year later, and nine months into the current clashes, Palestinian researchers found that 92 percent of Palestinians supported

---

[8] Statistics on wounded are minimum estimates based on Israeli official information and press accounts from the time; when the authorities' and press accounts varied, Human Rights Watch used the lower figure. No breakdown on the proportion of civilian vs. military is available for the wounded.

[9] The July 27-29, 2000 public opinion survey by the Palestinian Center for Policy and Survey Research showed an increase from the previous March from 44 to 52 percent of those who favored "violent confrontations" in the absence of an agreement on Palestinian statehood by the Oslo deadline of September 13, 2000. Palestinian Center for Policy and Survey Research, "Public Opinion Poll #1, Camp David Summit, Chances for Reconciliation and Lasting Peace, Violence and Confrontations, Hierarchies of Priorities, and Domestic Politics, 27-29 July 2000," www.pcpsr.org/survey/polls/2000/p1a, p. 4 (accessed August 29, 2002). In this and most other PCPSR polls, the questions did not distinguish between civilians or military targets. One poll that did, conducted in August-September 1995 by Palestinian Center for Policy and Survey Research, found that 70 percent of those questioned supported attacks on soldiers and settlers; 19 percent also favored attacks on residents of Israel and nearly 74 percent opposed such attacks. Palestinian Center for Policy and Survey Research "Public Opinion Poll # 19," http://www.pcpsr.org/survey/cprspolls/95/poll19a (accessed August 29, 2002).

armed confrontations against Israeli troops and 58 percent supported attacks against civilians inside Israel.[10] The same researchers found in a May 2002 survey that support for attacks against civilians in Israel had declined, but only to 52 percent.[11] Since May 2002, Palestinians have increasingly debated the use of suicide attacks against Israeli civilians, including the cumulative impact of such attacks on Palestinian society. (See below.)

Previous Use of Suicide Attacks Against Civilians

This is not the first time that Palestinian armed groups have used suicide bombings to target Israeli civilians, although the scale and intensity of the current wave of attacks is unprecedented. Between September 1993 and the outbreak of the latest clashes between Palestinians and Israelis in late September 2000, Palestinian groups carried out fourteen suicide bombing attacks against Israeli civilians, mostly in 1996-97, killing more than 120 and wounding over 550. [12] Hamas said it committed most of the attacks; Islamic Jihad claimed responsibility for the others.

The PA responded by detaining hundreds of Hamas and Islamic Jihad members and supporters, but they were not charged or brought to trial in connection with the bombings. Following these detentions, the bombings ceased. Many of the detainees, however, were released from PA custody once the clashes between Palestinians and Israelis resumed in September 2000.

---

[10] Palestinian Center for Policy and Survey Research, "Public Opinion Poll #2, The Mitchell Report, Cease Fire, and Return to Negotiations; Intifada and Armed Confrontations; Chances for Reconciliation; and, Internal Palestinian Conditions, 5-9 July 2001," www.pcpsr.org/survey/polls/2001/p2a (accessed August 29, 2002).

[11]Palestinian Center for Policy and Survey Research, "Public Opinion Poll #4, Palestinians Give Less Support For Bombings Inside Israel While Two Thirds Support The Saudi Plan And 91% Support Reforming The PA, But A Majority Opposes Arrests And Opposes The Agreements That Led To Ending The Siege On Arafat's Headquarter, Nativity Church, And Preventive Security Headquarter, 15-19 May 2002," at www.pcpsr.org/survey/polls/2002/p4a, p. 2 (accessed August 29, 2002). A different survey, by the Jerusalem Media and Communications Center in late May, indicated 68 percent (down from 72 percent) support for suicide bombings against civilians: Jerusalem Media and Communications Center, "JMCC Public Opinion Poll no. 45 - May 29- 31, June 1-2, 2002, On The Palestinian Attitudes Towards The Palestinian Situation in General" at http://www.jmcc.org/publicpoll/results/2002/index.htm (accessed August 29, 2002).

[12] Suicide bombing attacks against Israeli civilians in late February and early March 1996 killed fifty-six and injured more than 150. Five attacks in 1997 killed twenty-nine and wounded more than two hundred. The last suicide bombing prior to the current unrest was an attack in November 1998 that wounded twenty-four. There were no Palestinian suicide bomb attacks against civilians in 1999 or 2000.

Coincidentally or not, the new round of suicide bombings began within a few months, again under the auspices of Hamas and Islamic Jihad.

Various other groups around the world have also used suicide bombings to try to advance their political goals.[13] They include other Middle Eastern groups such as Hizbollah in Lebanon, which also attacked Israeli military targets and Israel's former proxy, the South Lebanese Army. But the group that has probably made greatest use of suicide bombings is the Tamil separatist group in Sri Lanka, the Liberation Tigers of Tamil Eelam (LTTE), commonly known as the "Tamil Tigers."[14] The Tamil Tigers committed numerous bombings during the 1980s and 1990s aimed at both military and civilian targets, including leading Sri Lankan government officials and politicians.

Stated Rationales for Suicide Bombing Attacks

Fathi 'Abd al-'Aziz al-Shikaki, one of Islamic Jihad's founders, was among the first to advocate openly the Palestinian use of bombing tactics against Israelis. In 1988, he publicly advocated a strategy of "exceptional" martyrdom according to which Palestinian militants would penetrate "enemy territory," that is, Israel, and set off explosions that the Israelis would be unable to prevent. According to al-Shikaki:

> All these results can be achieved through the explosion, which forces the *mujahid* (struggler) not to waver, not to escape, to execute a successful explosion for religion and jihad, and to destroy the morale of the enemy and plant terror into the people.[15]

Within Hamas, Yahya 'Ayyash, the organization's "master" bomb-maker, urged the leadership in the early 1990s to use "human bombs" as a way to "make the cost of the occupation that much more expensive in human lives, that

---

[13] For two discussions of suicide bombings more generally, see the essay by Navid Kermani ("A dynamite of the spirit: Why Nietzsche, not the Koran, is the key to understanding the suicide bombers,") in the *Times Literary Supplement* (March 29, 2002, pp. 13-15) and the review by Walter Lacquer, "Life as a weapon," also in the *TLS* (September 6, 2002, pp. 3-4).

[14] According to one report, the Liberation Tigers of Tamil Eelam (LTTE) has "dispatched more suicide bombers than anyone in the world," carrying out 220 suicide bomb attacks (Celia W. Dugger, "After ferocious fighting, Sri Lanka struggles with peace," *New York Times*, April 8, 2002). An LTTE suicide bomber also killed Indian Prime Minister Rajiv Gandhi.

[15] Nasra Hassan, "An Arsenal of Believers," *New Yorker*, November 19, 2001.

much more unbearable."[16] `Ayyash was killed by Israeli forces on January 5, 1996. Hamas claimed at the time that three suicide bombing attacks against Israeli civilians in late February and early March 1996 were in retaliation for the killing of `Ayyash.[17]

Leaders of the perpetrator groups have openly acknowledged that they favor suicide bombings because such attacks have the potential to cause a large number of casualties. They include civilians as well as military targets, in gross breach of their obligations under international humanitarian law. "The main thing is to guarantee that a large number of the enemy will be affected," said one senior Hamas leader. "With an explosive belt or bag, the bomber has control over vision, location, and timing."[18] Such weapons use readily available materials and are relatively inexpensive to produce.

The perpetrator organizations have also sought to use the bombings to build publicity for their cause, to drum up new recruits for suicide missions, and to sow anxiety and terror among Israelis. Before sending bombers on their suicide missions, the sponsoring organizations frequently had them make video testimonies that were then distributed and publicized through the media. The organizers sought to portray the bombers as "martyrs"—that is, as heroes prepared to make the ultimate sacrifice in defense of their people. In the same vein, they sought to compensate the bombers' families by providing some financial support. (See Section VI, Structures and Strategies of the Perpetrator Organizations.) In this way, those responsible for the bombings aimed to build an aura around the bombers and to exploit their actions even after their deaths. In fact, many of the bombers may have been motivated by a sense of personal self-sacrifice. However, their targeting of civilians, often using perfidious methods, made them and their sponsors, criminals. Their actions and disregard for basic human rights has tainted and undermined the wider struggle for Palestinian human rights.

Some suicide bombers, especially those sponsored by Hamas or Islamic Jihad, have cited Islam to justify their actions. Toward the same end, these organizations have invoked Muslim scholars and, through them, authoritative religious texts. Other prominent Muslim clerics have spoken against this invocation of religion to promote nationalist political goals. For Hamas and Islamic Jihad, the stated goal is the creation of a Palestinian Islamist state

---

[16] Ibid.

[17] Another Hamas suicide bombing on February 25, 1996, killed one IDF soldier and wounded thirty-four.

[18] Hassan, "An Arsenal...," *New Yorker.*

comprising not only the West Bank and Gaza Strip, but also the entire territory over which Israel has held sovereignty since 1948. The PFLP also calls for a Palestinian state encompassing Israel, though not an Islamist one. By contrast, the nationalist agenda of the al-Aqsa Martyrs' Brigades calls for establishing Palestinian rule over the territories of the West Bank and Gaza Strip and for freeing those territories from Israeli military occupation.

Victims

One factor that makes suicide bombing particularly terrifying is the sense that there is no possible shelter. Suicide bombers have targeted shopping malls, popular cafes and restaurants, quiet religiously observant neighborhoods, and commuter buses. Their target is everyday life.

Moti Mizrachi, mentioned earlier, had been a regular at the Moment Café. On March 9, he had agreed to meet friends at the fashionable cafe, like many other nights. Because of the crowd, the owner initially refused them access to the inside area, so Mizrachi and his friend waited outside for their turn to get in. Mizrachi told Human Rights Watch:

> At some point the owner moved away, and I said, "I'll just go inside to see my friends and say hi." I went in, took three to four steps and then there was an explosion. I fell to the floor. After a few seconds, I woke up. Everything around was torn apart. There was blood, body parts, people, water squirting from the ceiling, maybe from a burst pipe. My left hand was cut off just above the wrist. It was attached to my arm by just a bit of flesh, hanging. I picked myself up to get help. I was bleeding heavily. I know that I needed someone to stop the bleeding. I caught my left hand with my right, but I slipped from all the mess on the floor.[19]

Daniel Turjeman, a twenty-six-year-old patron, had two friends who were already inside. He and two others managed to convince the guard to let them in. It was so crowded that Turjeman and one friend went back outside, where they met a girl they knew.

> We greeted each other, and she introduced me to her girlfriend.... Just at that moment my friend came out, and before we had time to exchange even a word, everything exploded. We flew twenty meters

---

[19] Human Rights Watch interview with Moti Mizrachi, age thirty-one, Jerusalem, June 23, 2002.

from the blast, literally across the road, and fell onto the street. I lost consciousness and came to after a few minutes. There was screaming and ambulances. I felt that my arm was not connected to my body. It was barely connected to my shoulder. The friend who had invited me that evening came looking for me. He saw immediately that my arm was a mess. I also held one eye closed because it was full of metal. He asked me what was in his eye. I didn't want to tell him that his eye was hanging out, attached by just a few ligaments. It makes me sick to remember this.

There was such chaos there, people who were not badly injured were just getting into their cars and driving away, as quickly as possible. I knew I had to move or be run over. I caught my left arm, with the help of my jacket, and started making my way towards the ambulances. I had use of only one eye and couldn't see much, so I just kept walking towards the red lights.[20]

Turjeman's injuries include the loss of the use of one arm, ruptured eardrums, and a scratched cornea. He is recovering from temporary waist-down paralysis caused by hemorrhaging of his spine, and hopes to regain the use of both legs.

My friends who went out with me that night: one has a scratched cornea and is still full of shrapnel. He has pressure bandages for his arm, which was severely burned. He's suffering more than I am. My neighbor escaped without a scratch. My friend's two friends, one got a lot of nuts in his lower back, and was badly burned on his left side. The other fellow was killed. The girl who I spoke with outside had stepped into the bathroom at the time of the explosion, she survived. But the friend she introduced me to died.[21]

Efrat Ravid, age twenty, had been sitting at the bar at the Moment Café for two and a half hours when the explosion struck, shattering her thigh bone and causing a head injury. Unable to speak for a week after regaining consciousness, she now walks awkwardly with the aid of crutches. Her body is covered with scars. She doesn't smile.

---

[20] Human Rights Watch interview with Daniel Turjeman, age twenty-six, Jerusalem, June 23, 2002.

[21] Ibid.

We were at Moment for two and a half hours, sitting at the bar. Suddenly I heard a tremendous explosion and immediately blacked out. I must have blacked out from the pain, because my thighbone was broken into smithereens, and a major artery was ruptured. I had a serious head injury with hemorrhaging in the brain and stayed unconscious for three days....

When I woke up I understood right away what had happened. I couldn't talk at all then—for an entire week I couldn't talk, because my head injury was at the front of my brain. I stayed in the hospital for three months. My biggest fear was that they would amputate my leg—there were so many people in that hospital with missing limbs. They told me not to worry—they did an artery transplant, and said that even if it got infected later, there'd be enough time to do surgery. I've had ten operations since the attack. I also had a nail just a few millimeters from my heart. I think: what would have happened if it were just one millimeter over?

The friend I had been with was also injured—her intestines spilled right out. We don't talk any more. It brings up too many bad memories. The girl sitting on the other side of me—I didn't know her—she was killed. My friends don't go out any more. They realized when this happened to me; it could have been them. I had a lot of fears in the beginning. I still don't watch the news. When I do hear about an attack, it pinches me right in the heart. I know what it's like, I was there.[22]

Frequently, several family members are victims of an attack. Olesya Sorokin had immigrated to Israel in 2000 from Russia, with her husband and child. Her excitement over her opportunities in Israel ended on May 18, 2001, when a suicide bomber struck a shopping mall in Netanya.

My birthday had been on May 11, so we went to the mall to buy me a present: me, [my husband], my six-year-old son Sasha, and my friend Julia [Tritikov], my brother's girlfriend. I had only been there once before. It was before noon. We were at the entrance to the mall when there was a very loud "boom." I remember opening my eyes,

---

[22] Human Rights Watch interview with Efrat Ravid, age twenty, Ma'aleh Adumim, June 12, 2002.

half conscious. A doctor was looking over me, staring at me with big, frightened eyes. That's what it's like in a terror attack—people are in shock. People are lying, wounded, all around. I saw bones protruding from my foot. I could hear nothing. I have holes in my eardrums from the explosion. When I remember these moments, I just cry.[23]

Sorokin's husband and friend were killed in the attack; her son's jaw was broken, as was Sorokin's leg and jaw. Burns scarred her right arm, breast, and face. "I couldn't look into the mirror for the longest time. I've had many surgeries on my face—I don't go out because I'm not supposed to be in the sun, and because I'm embarrassed."[24] She said to Human Rights Watch:

What can I say. My soul is empty. I'm a widow at twenty-six. I have money now, from the Defense Ministry—an apartment ...but I want to return everything and get my husband back. I have no happiness. I don't laugh with my son. We had such a good relationship, my husband and I. We had dreams. I met him when I was seventeen and he was twenty-five. When I try to remember the life that I once had, I can't believe that all this happened. Maybe I'm sleeping. Maybe it didn't happen. Now I have to deal with life, alone. I know, I'm young, and there's time, but my head is full.[25]

Even when multiple family members are not directly affected, the entire family can be drawn into the tragic consequences. Clara Rosenberger, a seventy-six-year-old woman, was injured by shrapnel during an attack at the Park Hotel in Netanya during a Passover Seder on March 29, 2002. The friend she was with was killed. The shrapnel severed Rosenberger's spinal cord, leaving her bedridden; the blast also caused bleeding in her lungs and burst her eardrums. When Human Rights Watch saw her in the hospital, she barely communicated, sunken into her own world.[26] Her daughter described the impact it had had on her family.

---

[23] Human Rights Watch interview with Olesya Sorokin, age twenty-seven, Rishon Le Tzion, June 14, 2002.

[24] Ibid.

[25] Ibid.

[26] Human Rights Watch visits to Clara Rosenberger, Jerusalem, June 13, 2002 and June 23, 2002.

When she was first hospitalized, we were in the hospital day and night. That's something you don't hear about terror attacks. The victim's entire family becomes devoted exclusively to caring for the wounded. We were all involved—my brother, my children, my nieces and nephews, and me. The first hospital she was taken to was in Hadera, several hours north, and not where we live. Early on, her mental state deteriorated and she was transferred to a psychiatric hospital.... She's now in rehabilitation [in Jerusalem], but she still doesn't communicate much with visitors—doesn't read, or watch TV.... My children have been extremely helpful, but it is difficult for them to handle this and she's not easy to help. She cannot thank them, barely recognizes them. Her former life is over and her present life, she doesn't want it. It hurts so much—if only we could help her find something that gave her meaning.[27]

Clara Rosenberger had survived three and a half years as a prisoner in Auschwitz. Surviving members of the family split up, and Rosenberger came to Israel in 1947 as a war refugee. Her daughter told Human Rights Watch about Rosenberger's life and how it had been changed.

She was involved in all kinds of senior citizen's activities.... Now she is very dependent. She has no strength to deal with it—it was punishment enough that her life, with its tragedies, was as it was. She can't sit up because she is paralyzed from the underarms down, so she has no chest muscles. From the first moment we spoke after the attack, she said, "What happened to me was the very thing I did not want to happen to me, to be a burden on others." She won't ever be able to return home, she won't be able to live in her room.... Last week she was working on bringing a cup to her lips without it spilling. From total independence to this.[28]

By targeting public places, suicide bombings affect all sectors of Israeli society, not only Israeli Jews. Lin Jin Mou was a Chinese construction worker who came to Israel on a legal visa, supporting a family at home with his modest income. On April 12, 2002, he was boarding a bus with three friends at the Mahane Yehuda open-air market in Jerusalem when a suicide bomber blew up

---

[27] Human Rights Watch interview with Rachel Klirs, daughter of Clara Rosenberger, Jerusalem, July 2, 2002.

[28] Ibid.

the bus. Ben Tsion Maltabashi, a sixty-five-year-old man whose leg had to be amputated, was also there and described what happened:

> There are a lot of buses that come to that stop: the 27, 13, 11, 39, and others. I saw [my bus] and thought, "Great, I'll go right home." There was a line onto the bus. I stood in line—there were tons of people. Everyone was going home on account of the Sabbath. One got on, then another, then another, and then "boom." As if the entire roof fell on my head.[29]

Lin lost his left arm and his left leg, which was amputated because of severe burns. Two of his friends who had already boarded were among the six killed in that attack.[30]

Sabrina Belhadev, a French citizen in Israel on a study-abroad program, was visiting Jerusalem with friends for a weekend on December 1, 2001, when two Palestinians blew themselves up moments apart near a row of packed cafés on Jerusalem's Ben Yehuda pedestrian mall, killing ten and wounding more than 170.

> I didn't understand what happened. Everyone was screaming, 'Run, run—there may be another bomber here,' but I didn't have the strength. There was an enormous confusion and mess. Chairs and tables were strewn everywhere. Everyone was crying. There was someone I saw passed out in a chair, and there was blood coming out of his head; I think he was dead. And people drenched in blood.[31]

Belhadev's friend, Eva Krief, a fellow French student on the study-abroad program, escaped the suicide bombing attacks inside the café, but was injured by a car bomb when she tried to leave the scene. "A few minutes after [Sabrina] entered the café, there was an explosion. It felt like an earthquake. It wasn't that the noise was so loud—just the destruction. I was stunned. I forgot about my friends. I didn't understand what had happened at all." Krief walked another

[29] Human Rights Watch interview with Ben Tsion Maltabashi, age sixty-five, Jerusalem, June 13, 2002,

[30] Human Rights Watch interview with Li Yuan Wong, age twenty-eight, assistant to Lin Jin Mou, age forty-one, Jerusalem, June 23, 2002.

[31] Human Rights Watch interview with Sabrina Belhadev, age twenty, Jerusalem, June 17, 2002.

friend, who had a head wound, to an ambulance and met a third friend, who suggested going back to the dormitory.

> So we decided to go up a side street—HaRav Kook. On our way up the street, a car bomb exploded from a parking space off the side. I was struck in the leg—not by shrapnel, but some other flying object—and in my left eye. My hair was also quite singed, though I only noticed this later. Everything was hot, hot.[32]

Krief permanently lost the sight in her left eye. "I am quite afraid now," she said. She explained to Human Rights Watch:

> It began in the hospital—every slamming door, every noise scared me. I'm slowly getting back to life, but it's been very hard. I'm afraid of going on the bus, afraid of going out. When I hear about attacks every few days, on the news… everything comes back. It's one thing if you're in an attack, and you recuperate, and there are no more. But they keep happening.[33]

Krief said that she had previously been undecided about whether she might stay in Israel or return to France. "Since my injury it is clear to me that I have to stay here. I can't say why, but due to what has happened, this is my place, more than ever."[34]

Palestinian Arab citizens of Israel have also been victims of bomb attacks. Hussam Abu Hussein had taken his sixteen-month-old daughter to Hadera for an outing on November 22, 2000.

> When we arrived, she started asking for pizza. She likes to eat it with ketchup—more for the fun than for the flavor. I took her to a pizza place where I know the owners.... I was sitting in the pizzeria—my daughter was in my arms. Suddenly, I found myself somewhere and the child was somewhere else. I thought a gas balloon had blown up. Everywhere was filled with dark smoke. I tasted something bad in my mouth. Thick smoke. The smell of burning flesh in my mouth. I

---

[32] Human Rights Watch interview with Eva Krief, age twenty, Jerusalem, July 5, 2002.

[33] Ibid.

[34] Ibid.

didn't know what it was. I remember everything because I didn't faint. I saw someone without legs—they were burned away. I was stunned—I forgot that my daughter had been with me. Suddenly I remembered. I went to find her. She was inside a ball of fire.[35]

Hussam Abu Hussein then ran into the street.

I realized there had been a terror attack. And I was afraid. Afraid because I am an Arab—that someone would think I had done it. I climbed into an ambulance and put my hand over my daughter's mouth so that she wouldn't scream and draw attention to us. I kept telling the driver, "Go! Go! Now! Go!" It later turned out that I had run 100 meters with a metal dowel in my back—it must have lodged in there when the bus blew up, maybe part of the bus.[36]

Hussam Abu Hussein and his daughter were both badly burned in this attack, which killed two and wounded fifty. According to Abu Hussein, his daughter's hair now does not grow normally, and the skin grafts she received to treat her burns have caused extensive scarring on her neck and the back of her left hand, "like the hand of an eighty year old woman," he described it. The two also suffer psychologically. "I suffer from nightmares. I wake up sweating, no matter how high I turn on the air conditioner. My daughter wakes up too, in the middle of the night, shouting, 'No, no, no.'"

Abu Hussein told Human Rights Watch:

How do I deal with this as a Palestinian? It's not easy. They [in the West Bank and Gaza] suffer—more than anybody. But when someone hurts you, you're angry. It doesn't matter if it's your mother, father, cousin, brother. When someone tries to kill you, you don't "understand" them. You don't care what their problem was at the moment—what their reason was, what they're suffering. As long as the damage is far from me, I'll try to understand. But when it's my body, my child—I'm angry. That's my immediate response. God gave life, and no one but God has the right to take it. This isn't the

---

[35] Human Rights Watch interview with Hussam Abu Hussein, Baka al-Gharbiya, June 26, 2002.

[36] Ibid.

way to conduct ourselves—on both sides. Violence never works—I strike you, you strike me —there's no end. It will solve nothing.[37]

Attacks

Since attacks against civilians resumed on January 1, 2001, the number of suicide bombings has increased dramatically.

They have become the type of attack that Israeli civilians expect and fear from Palestinian armed groups. March 2001 saw three attacks that killed five and wounded ninety. Another series of suicide bombings and a car bombing in the second half of May 2001 were eclipsed on June 1, 2001, when twenty-two-year-old Said Hutari blew himself up amidst a crowd of Israeli teenagers outside a popular Tel Aviv nightclub, the Dolphinarium.[38]

The Dolphinarium attack, the deadliest suicide bombing in more than four years, immediately killed seventeen, almost all of them recent immigrants from the former Soviet Union, and wounded between eighty-five and ninety. The death toll climbed to twenty-one over the following days. The Tel Aviv police chief, Commander Yossi Sedbon, said the bomb, though not large, had been filled with nails, screws, and ball bearings.[39] Islamic Jihad at first claimed responsibility, but then deferred to a subsequent claim by Hamas.[40]

President Arafat condemned the attack, which came as Israeli and Palestinian security officials resumed talks under U.S. auspices on implementing the recommendations of the report by the Sharm el-Sheikh Fact-Finding Committee, headed by former U.S. Senator George Mitchell. For the first time since clashes erupted, and under intense international pressure, Arafat publicly called for an immediate and unconditional cease-fire.[41]

---

[37] Ibid.

[38] The Associated Press reported that four car bombs over the previous week had "failed to cause casualties." Dan Perry, "Tel Aviv suicide bombing kills 17 Israelis," Associated Press, June 2, 2001.

[39] Allyn Fisher-Ilan, "Five from one school dead in attack; others saved by a 'twist of fate,'" *Jerusalem Post*, June 3, 2001.

[40] `Ala'a Saftawi, former editor-in-chief of the pro-Islamic Jihad weekly newspaper *Al-Istiqlal*, told Human Rights Watch that Hamas was responsible for the Dolphinarium attack. Human Rights Watch interview, Gaza City, May 15, 2002. News reports also cited Hamas' claims of responsibility for the attack. See Ewen MacAskill, "Arafat refuses to arrest bombers: Palestinian leader voices respect for extremist groups but warns of future roundup," *Guardian* (London), June 30, 2001. Some news reports at the time said that a previously unknown group, Palestinian Hizbollah, had also claimed responsibility.

[41] German Foreign Minister Joschka Fischer was in Ramallah at the time and, along with U.N. Special Coordinator Terje Larsen, worked with Arafat to draft the statement. Fatah

However, suicide bombings continued in July, August, and September. In the most notorious of these, a bomber entered a crowded Sbarro pizzeria at the busy intersection of Jaffa Road and King George Avenue in Jerusalem and detonated a bomb packed with nails, screws, and bolts. The blast gutted the restaurant, crowded with lunchtime diners, killing fifteen and wounding more than 130. "I cannot even describe in words the horror of it all," said one witness, who worked next door. "They were bringing the bodies of the wounded into our shop—children, women, covered in blood."[42] Islamic Jihad was the first to claim responsibility, but Hamas subsequently took credit, saying the bomber was twenty-three-year-old 'Izz al-Din al-Masri.[43]

The PA made several arrests in the wake of this attack, detaining the alleged driver and three other Hamas militants, including 'Abdallah Barghouti, the person Israel said had dispatched al-Masri.[44] President Arafat also fired Ramallah police chief Kamal al-Shaikh for allowing armed youths to celebrate the attack and ordered the closure of an exhibit erected several weeks later in Nablus by Hamas students at an-Najah University celebrating the attack.[45]

President Arafat made a well-publicized call for an end to attacks in mid-November 2001, and the PA reportedly made arrests and closed down several

---

agreed to comply with Arafat's call, but Hamas, Islamic Jihad, and the Popular Front for the Liberation of Palestine pointedly did not. George Tenet, director of the U.S. Central Intelligence Agency, negotiated a cease-fire agreement that was announced on June 13, 2001. Some Palestinian Authority-Israeli security contacts were re-established, and the number of serious incidents of Palestinian violence declined for several weeks. On June 23, 2001, the Palestinian Authority reportedly detained Islamic Jihad leader 'Abdallah Shami in Gaza for "acting against Palestinian interests" in criticizing the cease-fire. By mid-July, however, the level of violence initiated by Palestinians and Israelis had returned to that which prevailed prior to the Dolphinarium attack. On June 22 and July 16, 2001, Hamas and Islamic Jihad respectively carried out suicide bombing attacks that killed four IDF soldiers in Gaza and Binyamina and wounded ten others.

[42] Etgar Lefkowitz, "Fifteen killed in Jerusalem suicide bombing; cabinet deliberates retaliation for attack," *Jerusalem Post*, August 10, 2001.

[43] For a detailed account of the preparations for this attack and a portrait of al-Masri and his accomplices, see Sarah Helm, "The Human Time Bomb," *Sunday Times Magazine*, January 6, 2002.

[44] Alan Philips, "Arafat's arrest of militants fails to halt the 'martyrs,'" *Daily Telegraph*, August 13, 2001. Other reports identified two of those detained as 'Abdallah and Bilal Barghouti.

[45] On Ramallah, see "Israeli soldiers close further building as U.S. envoy starts talks," Deutsche Presse-Agentur, August 12, 2001; on Nablus, see "Arafat Closes 'Suicide Bombing' Art Show", BBC online news, 26 September 2001 at http://news.bbc.co.uk/1/hi/entertainment/arts/1564188.stm (accessed August 29, 2002).

dozen charities and similar institutions affiliated with Islamist organizations.[46] However, these initiatives were followed by six suicide attacks on civilians in the first two weeks of December, killing twenty-nine and wounding close to two hundred.

The first days of December 2001 witnessed bombings in Jerusalem and Haifa that killed twenty-five and wounded hundreds. On the night of Saturday, December 1, 2001, two Palestinians blew themselves up moments apart near a row of packed cafés on Jerusalem's Ben Yehuda pedestrian mall, killing ten and wounding more than 170. Some twenty minutes later, a block away, a car bomb exploded. Michel Haroush, a French tourist, told reporters, "I fell down, and next thing I saw was half a human body lying by my foot."[47] Another witness, Yossi Mizrahi, said, "I saw people without arms. I saw a person with their stomach hanging open. I saw a ten-year-old boy breathe his last breath. I can't believe anybody would do anything like this."[48]

Scarcely twelve hours later, at midday on December 2, 2001, a young Palestinian blew himself up in a crowded Haifa city bus, killing fifteen and wounding three dozen. *Washington Post* reporter Lee Hockstader described the scene:

> In an instant, the bus became an inferno of death and blood. Corpses and fragments of bodies were strewn across the seats and aisles, and the wounded staggered out the doors and tumbled from the shattered windows. The bomb tore apart students and retirees, Filipino workers and Russian immigrants, soldiers and civilians—a random sampling of this working-class city's diverse population.[49]

Hamas claimed responsibility for the attack. Its leaflet called the Jerusalem and Haifa bombings "the natural retaliation by a people slaughtered day and

---

[46] On November 16, 2001, in a televised speech in Arabic marking the end of Ramadan, Yasir Arafat called for "the complete cessation of all military activities, especially suicide attacks, which we have always condemned," adding that the PA would "punish all planners and executors and hunt down the violators." Graham Usher, "Entering the storm," *Middle East International*, December 21, 2001, p. 7.

[47] Tracy Wilkinson, "Suicide bombers strike in heart of Jerusalem," *Los Angeles Times*, December 2, 2001.

[48] Ibid.

[49] Lee Hockstader, "Bomber on bus kills fifteen in Israel," *Washington Post*, December 3, 2001.

night, whose dignity is humiliated by the Zionist enemy's war machine."[50] Islamic Jihad claimed responsibility for two other attacks during this period.

Palestinian officials, while denouncing the attacks on Israeli civilians, implicitly sought to justify them by pointing to the provocative impact of incidents such as an alleged Israeli booby-trap bomb that killed five young boys in Khan Yunis on November 22, 2001. "Everyone should realize that atrocities lead to atrocities," said Nabil Sha'ath, the PA minister of planning and international cooperation. "This is the inevitable outcome of the accumulation of atrocities committed by the Israeli army against our civilians, the humiliation, the torment, the unmitigated persecution," Sha'ath said.[51]

On December 21, 2001, following clashes with PA security forces that left seven Palestinians dead and scores injured, Hamas's `Izz al-Din al-Qassam Brigades issued a leaflet announcing that it would "suspend" attacks within "land occupied since 1948"—i.e. Israel. Battles with guns and clubs had broken out when PA security forces attempted to arrest `Abd al-`Aziz al-Rantisi, a senior Hamas leader. Eventually al-Rantisi agreed to "a form of house arrest" and to refrain from issuing public statements.[52] Arafat told the Israeli daily, *Ha'aretz,* on December 21 that securing the Hamas statement "wasn't easy, and the declaration came after we pressured them." The PA's campaign did produce a month, from December 16 until January 17, with no attacks against civilians inside Israel.[53]

The respite for Israeli civilians was not to last. On January 17, 2002, three days after the assassination of local al-Aqsa Martyrs' Brigades leader Ra'id al-Karmi, twenty-seven-year-old Ahmad Hassouna killed six Israelis and wounded thirty when he attacked a bat mitzvah celebration in Hadera with an assault rifle and grenades.[54] The al-Aqsa Brigades also claimed a second shooting attack, in

---

[50] Ibid.

[51] Khalid Amayreh, "Pushing Arafat into a corner," *Middle East International,* December 7, 2001, p. 5.

[52] The *Jerusalem Post* cited an unnamed "senior Israeli official" as dismissing the PA effort: "Rantisi is a symbol and the least of the real terrorists. And these people [Arafat] is not arresting. He is going for the symbols." Lamia Lahoud, "Hamas, Fatah strike deal to prevent Rantisi's arrest," *Jerusalem Post,* December 22, 2001.

[53] During the lull, shooting attacks against Israeli military targets and settlements continued. The break on attacks inside Israel was interrupted from the Palestinian side when Hamas militants ambushed and killed four Israeli soldiers in Israel near the Gaza border on January 9, 2002. Israel the next day destroyed some fifty-nine homes in Gaza's Rafah refugee camp.

[54] Graham Usher, "Six Shot Dead at Bat Mitzvah," *Guardian* (London), January 18, 2002.

downtown Jerusalem on January 22. Two civilians were killed, including a seventy-eight-year-old woman, and fourteen were injured.[55]

On January 27, 2002, twenty-six-year-old Wafa' Idris from al-Amari refugee camp, killed an eighty-one-year-old man and wounded over one hundred in downtown Jerusalem. This first suicide bombing attack claimed by the al-Aqsa Martyrs' Brigades was also the first in which a woman was the perpetrator.[56] Though hardly a justification, the al-Aqsa Brigades' adoption of suicide bombing tactics and attacks against civilians inside Israel reflected at least in part a growing fear by Fatah that it was losing political ground to the Islamist groups that had been carrying out such attacks, especially Hamas. "When the al-Aqsa Brigades started [suicide bombing] operations, it was the decision of all districts," one Fatah leader in the Jenin refugee camp told Human Rights Watch. "The political leaders feared they would lose their influence in the street and in the [National and Islamic Forces] Front. The push of Israeli policies is to shift all influence [in Palestinian armed groups] from the political [wing] to the military." [57]

The number of attacks continued to mount. In March 2002, twelve suicide bombings of civilian targets killed some eighty civilians and injured more than 450. The al-Aqsa Martyrs' Brigades claimed responsibility for five of these attacks, Hamas for three, Islamic Jihad for three, and the PFLP for one.[58] The

---

[55] "Ceasefire Offer Follows Bus Stop Attack," *Guardian* (London), January 23, 2002.

[56] In Lebanon, Hizbollah's al-Manar television first claimed, on behalf of Hamas, that the bomber was a twenty-year-old woman student from al-Najah University in Nablus. Hamas leader Shaikh Yassin later said that "in this phase, the participation of women is not needed in martyr operations like men." See "We don't need women suicide bombers: Hamas spiritual leader," Agence France-Presse, February 2, 2002. A second suicide bombing attack carried out by a woman, and also claimed by the al-Aqsa Martyrs' Brigades, wounded three Israeli police at a checkpoint on February 27, 2002.

[57] Interview with `Ata Abu Rumaila, Jenin refugee camp, June 11, 2002. An official in the PA General Intelligence Service told Human Rights Watch, "When the al-Aqsa Brigades responded to Karmi's assassination—this was not a political decision on the level of the central committee. We were shocked. I knew what the Palestinian answer would be—not Arafat's or Fatah's, but the friends and neighbors. And what I expected happened." Human Rights Watch interview, Ramallah, June 5, 2002. A Western security official involved in security negotiations in 2001-2002 told Human Rights Watch, "the December-January cease-fire was effective because it was informal and locally based.... The [Israeli] assassinations have been timed to destroy cease-fires." Human Rights Watch interview, Jerusalem, June 6, 2002.

[58] The March 7 attack by the PFLP on a hotel on the outskirts of Ariel settlement wounded fifteen. The other PFLP suicide bombing attack, on February 16, killed three and wounded more than thirty in a pizzeria in the Karnei Shomron settlement.

Hamas attack during a Passover Seder in Netanya's Park Hotel was the deadliest, killing twenty-nine civilians, many elderly, and injuring one hundred.

The March 2002 attacks began just after 7:00 p.m. on the evening of March 2, when a bomber blew himself up in a car among ultra-Orthodox worshippers as they streamed onto the street in the Me'ah Shearim neighborhood of west Jerusalem following prayers marking the end of the Sabbath. The blast killed eleven, including four children from one family—one a baby girl. More than fifty were wounded. Palestinian security sources identified the bomber as Muhammad Daraghmeh, a seventeen-year-old from Dheisheh refugee camp near Bethlehem. The al-Aqsa Martyrs' Brigades claimed responsibility.[59]

On Saturday night, March 9, 2002, Fu'ad Hourani, a twenty-year-old from al-Arroub refugee camp near Hebron, stepped into Café Moment and detonated a powerful bomb that killed eleven and wounded more than fifty. (See victim testimonies above.) A Hamas statement claimed responsibility for it as "a brave attack... to avenge the Israeli massacres against our people."[60] The Café Moment bombing came two hours after two Palestinians opened fire and tossed grenades at a seafront hotel in Netanya, killing a baby and one other person and wounding more than thirty. The perpetrators of that attack, responsibility for which was claimed by the al-Aqsa Martyrs' Brigades, were killed in a shootout with Israeli police.

Another suicide bombing occurred on March 20, 2002, aboard Bus No. 283 near Umm al-Fahm, in the Galilee region, killing four soldiers and three civilians. Fifteen of the twenty-nine wounded were not Jewish but Palestinian Arab citizens of Israel. The perpetrator was twenty-four-year-old Rafat Abu Diyak, from the town of Jenin. The Islamic Jihad organization claimed responsibility. Bus No. 283 had been attacked by suicide bombers twice before, in Afula on March 5, 2002 and near Pardes Hanna on November 29, 2001. (See Appendix One.)

The next day, March 21, 2002, the al-Aqsa Martyrs' Brigades claimed credit for a suicide bombing on a crowded shopping street in Jerusalem that killed three and wounded at least sixty. Al-Aqsa Martyrs' Brigades sources reportedly confirmed Israeli allegations that the perpetrator, a twenty-two-year-

---

[59] Some reports give Daraghmeh's age as twenty and his full name as Muhammad Daraghmeh Ashouani; Human Rights Watch uses the name and age as given by his family.

[60] "Hamas claims responsibility for Jerusalem bombing," Reuters, March 9, 2002.

old former policeman, had at one time been detained by PA security forces but was released during the Israeli incursions into Ramallah earlier in March.[61]

The deadliest single Palestinian suicide bombing attack occurred on March 27, 2002, when twenty-five-year-old `Abd al-Basit `Awdah, a Hamas activist from Tulkarem, blew himself up in a Netanya hotel as some 250 people sat down to a Passover Seder. The blast killed at least nineteen Israelis immediately and wounded scores of others; the death toll later climbed to twenty-nine. Clara Rosenberger, one of the many people badly injured in the blast (see above), had chosen to attend the hotel Seder specifically because there had been a shooting attack in Netanya several weeks earlier and she had wanted to feel safe.[62] Entire families were reportedly among those killed and wounded, including some visiting from elsewhere.

Palestinian sources confirmed that the PA had earlier detained `Awdah at the request of Israel, but only briefly.[63]

The perpetrators of the March attacks generally tried to justify them as retaliation for Israeli abuses, or as legitimate acts of resistance. Mahmud al-Titi, for example, an al-Aqsa Martyrs' Brigades leader in Balata refugee camp near Nablus, said on March 8, "While [Israeli forces] were attacking Balata refugee camp, our groups in Bethlehem were preparing retaliation."[64] Hamas, the main

---

[61] "Suicide Bomb Stalls Mideast Peace Talks," *Boston Globe*, March 22, 2002.

[62] Human Rights Watch interview with Rachel Klirs, daughter of Clara Rosenberger, Jerusalem, July 2, 2002.

[63] "Israeli source says Netanya bombing 'declaration of war', 20 dead," BBC Monitoring Middle East, March 28, 2002. According to the *Jerusalem Report*, an Israeli biweekly, `Awdah joined Hamas after Israeli security forces had prevented him from crossing the Allenby bridge to Amman to marry his fiancée prior to the intifada. See Khaled Abu Toameh, "Love and Hate," *Jerusalem Report*, May 20, 2002, p. 27. Ya'ov Limor, writing in the daily *Ma'ariv* on August 17, 2001, many months before the Netanya attack, reported that Nahid Abu Ishaq, a Hamas activist detained by the Israeli Defense Force in connection with the Sbarro pizzeria bombing in Jerusalem, "was found in possession of the last testament of Basit `Awdah, who was about to carry out another suicide attack," in "Terror map of Hamas and Islamic Jihad," *Ma'ariv*, translated in Foreign Broadcast Information Service (FBIS), Near East and South Asia, August 20, 2001, FBIS-NES-2001-0817. At around that time it appears that `Awdah went underground. He was reportedly on the list of persons sought by Israeli forces during the IDF incursion into Tulkarem in January 2002, but escaped capture at that time. (The IDF raid on Tulkarem is discussed in Human Rights Watch, "In a Dark Hour: The Use of Civilians during IDF Arrest," *A Human Rights Watch Report*, vol. 14, no. 2 (E), April 2002, pp. 16-19.)

[64] Mohammed Daraghmeh, "Militia leader seeks to build Palestinian liberation arm," Associated Press, March 8, 2002. Al-Titi said in the same interview, "I believe that they have put me on the assassination list. So, sooner or later they are going to assassinate me, so I'll kill them, as many as I can." Al-Titi and three others were killed when an Israeli tank targeted them on May 22, 2002.

Palestinian opposition group, said that its attacks were also intended to disrupt moves towards political negotiations. A Hamas statement claimed that one purpose of the Netanya Park Hotel Passover Seder attack was to derail diplomatic initiatives at an Arab League summit in Beirut. "The summit resolutions are below the aspirations and the sacrifices of the Palestinian people," said `Usama Hamdan, a Hamas spokesman in Beirut.[65]

The Palestinian Authority agreed that "this operation against Israeli civilians is in essence an attack against the Arab summit and against [U.S. Special Representative Anthony] Zinni's mission." It went on to say that "the leadership strongly denounces any endangering of Palestinian or Israeli civilians and will not practice leniency with parties claiming responsibility and will take firm measures to bring those responsible before a court."[66]

President Yasir Arafat routinely condemned these suicide bombing attacks against civilians. Following the March 2 attack, the PA issued a statement saying that it "denounces strongly and unambiguously any operations targeting civilians whether Israelis or Palestinians, including the operation executed this evening, Saturday, March 2, 2002, in the center of a civilian neighborhood in Jerusalem"[67] Arafat also condemned the March 21 al-Aqsa Martyrs' Brigades attack against "innocent Israeli civilians." "We will take the appropriate and immediate measures to put an end to such attacks," he said.[68]

Seeming public justifications of the bombings, however, came from figures close to Arafat, especially after the al-Aqsa Martyrs' Brigades began carrying out suicide bombing attacks against civilians in early 2002. Ahmad `Abd al-Rahman, an Arafat advisor and secretary of the PA Cabinet, responded to the March 9, 2002 attack on the Café Moment in Jerusalem by saying: "This is the normal response from the Palestinian resistance for all the Israelis have done in the refugee camps, to Palestinian civilians, women and children.... The Israelis have to expect such operations whenever they escalate their military attacks

---

[65] Hussein Dakroub, "Militant Palestinian Groups Reject Arab Peace Overture to Israel," Associated Press, March 28, 2002.

[66] "The leadership strongly denounces Netanya operation against Israeli civilians and decides to prosecute those involved or responsible, " WAFA (official PA news agency), March 27, 2002. Translated from Arabic by Human Rights Watch.

[67] "The Palestinian Authority denounces any operations targeting Palestinian and Israeli civilians, " WAFA (official PA news agency), March 2, 2002. Translated from Arabic by Human Rights Watch.

[68] "Suicide Bomb Stalls Mideast Peace Talks," *Boston Globe*, March 22, 2002.

against our civilians."[69] Marwan Barghouti, the West Bank general secretary of Fatah, wrote in January 2002 that he, "and the Fatah movement to which I belong, strongly oppose attacks and the targeting of civilians inside Israel, our future neighbor...."[70] But following the March 21 al-Aqsa Martyrs' Brigades suicide bombing on a crowded Jerusalem shopping street that killed three and wounded sixty, Barghouti commented to reporters, "Our people have resorted to resistance because we have reached an impasse. The more the Israelis tighten the blockades around us and increase the killing, the more there will be a response."[71]

Despite the sometimes equivocal condemnations of the PA leadership, the al-Aqsa Martyrs' Brigades' suicide bombings did not stop. Just before 2:00 p.m. on March 29, an eighteen-year-old woman from Dheisheh refugee camp outside Bethlehem, Ayat Muhammad al-'Akhras, detonated an explosive belt she was wearing in a supermarket in the Jerusalem suburb of Kiryat Hayovel. The blast killed two and wounded more than twenty. Al-'Akhras reportedly carried an explosive device in her handbag that failed to explode. The al-Aqsa Martyrs' Brigades claimed responsibility. Al-'Akhras, in a pre-recorded videotape, condemned Arab leaders for "watching while Palestinian women" fought the Israeli occupation.[72]

In Operation Defensive Shield, beginning at the end of March 2002, Israeli forces re-occupied most of the Palestinian-controlled "Area A" of the West Bank, which included the major Palestinian population centers apart from East Jerusalem and about 18 percent of the total area.[73] The Israeli operation did not stop suicide bombings, although the pace of the attacks dropped. On March 30, at 9:30 p.m., a suicide bombing attack in a central Tel Aviv restaurant wounded some twenty people, one of whom eventually died. The al-Aqsa Martyrs' Brigades identified the perpetrator as twenty-three-year-old Muhannad Ibrahim Salahat, from the village of al-Faraa, near Nablus. In the first of two attacks on March 31, 2002, a suicide bomber seriously wounded three people near a volunteer medic station in Efrat, one of the Gush Etzion bloc settlements near

---

[69] Greg Myre, "Israel destroys Arafat's Gaza office after suicide bombing in Jerusalem," Associated Press, March 10, 2002.

[70] "Want Security? End the Occupation," *Washington Post,* January 16, 2002.

[71] "Suicide Bomb Stalls Mideast Peace Talks," *Boston Globe*, March 22, 2002.

[72] "Suicide bomber kills two in Jerusalem supermarket," Reuters, March 29, 2002.

[73] For a detailed account of one component of this operation, see Human Rights Watch, "Jenin: IDF Military Operations," *A Human Rights Watch Report,* vol. 14, no. 3 (E), May 2002.

Bethlehem. The al-Aqsa Martyrs' Brigades named the perpetrator as Jamal Hamaid, seventeen years old, from Bethlehem. The same day, Hamas took responsibility for an attack in Haifa in which twenty-three-year-old Shadi Abu Tubassi from Jenin refugee camp killed fifteen and wounded more than thirty when he blew himself up in a restaurant crowded with Israeli citizens, both Jewish and Palestinian Arab.

The first suicide bombing after the Israel Defense Forces (IDF) operation had ended, in a pool hall in Rishon Letzion on May 7, 2002, killed fifteen and wounded fifty. The Palestinian Authority issued a statement saying that it "promptly condemns the violent attack against Israeli civilians" and said that it had "decided to take effective measures against those involved in this dangerous operation and those who are standing behind it. And we will not go easy with these groups...."[74] President Arafat, in a televised address the next day, said, "I gave my orders and directions to all the Palestinian security forces to confront and prevent all terror attacks against Israeli civilians from any Palestinian side or parties."[75] In response to initial reports that the perpetrator was affiliated with Hamas and may have come from Gaza, PA security forces rounded up more than a dozen rank-and-file Hamas members there.[76] In the following days, Israeli forces killed two Palestinian security officers in Halhoul and arrested others elsewhere in the West Bank, but these were apparently not persons wanted in connection with the Rishon Letzion bombing.[77]

During May and June 2002, Palestinian militants carried out nine suicide bombings and made numerous attempts that were thwarted. The al-Aqsa Martyrs' Brigades claimed responsibility for five of the nine attacks. The first was carried out by Jihad al-Titi, a nephew of prominent al-Aqsa Martyrs' Brigades leader Mahmud al-Titi. The attack immediately followed Israel's assassination of Mahmud al-Titi in Balata camp.[78] A statement from al-Aqsa Martyrs' Brigades called suicide attacks its "sole weapon to end the

---

[74] Statement as published in the *New York Times*, May 8, 2002.

[75] Greg Myre, "Palestinians arrest Hamas members; Bethlehem talks break down," Associated Press, May 9, 2002.

[76] Phil Reeves, "Arafat tries to stave off Gaza assault with arrests," *The Independent* (London), May 10, 2002.

[77] For a detailed account of the killings in Halhoul, see Edward Cody, "Israel pursues focused attacks: In killing of West Bank intelligence agents, a pattern resumes," *Washington Post*, May 16, 2002.

[78] Three other persons, two of them al-Aqsa Martyrs' Brigades members, were also killed by the Israeli tank shell that killed al-Titi. Israel asserted that al-Titi was responsible for the deaths of at least eleven Israelis, mostly in attacks employing automatic weapons.

occupation."[79] In an attempted attack two days later, an Israeli security guard shot and killed the driver of a car loaded with pipe bombs as the car sped towards a crowded Tel Aviv nightclub.[80]

Hamas and the PFLP claimed joint responsibility for a May 19 attack on a Netanya outdoor market. The perpetrator, dressed as a soldier, killed an elderly man and a teenage boy and wounded dozens. Hamas also claimed responsibility for two other suicide attacks, including an attack on a bus traveling from the Israeli settlement of Gilo to Jerusalem on June 18, 2002, which killed nineteen and wounded at least seventy-four. The al-Aqsa Martyrs' Brigades claimed responsibility for an attack the following day at a bus stop near the French Hill settlement in East Jerusalem.

On June 20, in response to these attacks, the IDF launched "Operation Determined Path," in which it again re-occupied seven out of eight major Palestinian West Bank cities. Prime Minister Sharon said, "This is not occupation, but we will remain in Palestinian areas for as long as necessary to carry out essential operations."[81] On August 20, IDF troops staged a negotiated withdrawal from Bethlehem, on condition that PA Security forces would prevent future armed activities there.[82]

Martyrdom, Public Officials, and the Role of the Media
Public statements by officials have delivered mixed messages on suicide attacks. Palestinian officials, as noted above, have frequently condemned suicide attacks against civilians. But Palestinian and regional officials have also made statements that support and, at times, promote them. Israeli authorities and critics of the PA have also argued that Palestinian media have fostered public support for such attacks.

Media in the Occupied Territories consist of local, privately funded television and radio; PA-funded television and radio; and satellite channels broadcast from surrounding countries, including *al-Manar,* affiliated with the Lebanese movement Hizbollah. Of three major Palestinian newspapers, *al-Ayyam* and *al-Hayat al-Jadedah* are published in the West Bank and *al-Quds* is published in East Jerusalem after clearance by the Israeli military censor. Many

---

[79] John Kifner, "Israel thwarts bomb attack, but fears more to come," *New York Times,* May 25, 2002.

[80] The encounter set off a blast that injured one person.

[81] Gil Hoffman and Margot Dudkevitch, "Sharon: Massive Assault on Hamas Underway in Gaza," *Jerusalem Post,* June 25, 2002.

[82] Serge Schmeann, "Israel Will Start Pullout in Gaza and Bethlehem," *New York Times,* August 19, 2002. As of late September, the IDF pullout has been limited to Bethlehem.

residents of the Occupied Territories also have access to Israeli television, radio, and print media, in both Arabic and Hebrew. As curfews and limits on movement have become increasingly restrictive, the importance of media—and particularly television—as the primary source of public information has increased. Palestinian and Arabic regional media outlets have followed the events of the Israeli-Palestinian clashes closely, and the degree of media coverage reflects the immense impact that the clashes have had on Palestinian and Arab society.

Israeli and other critics have argued that the Palestinian media contribute to suicide attacks on civilians by placing an inappropriate, commendatory emphasis on martyrdom. The concept of martyrdom—of sacrifice for the sake of one's beliefs or principles—is neither exclusively Muslim nor exclusively religious. In the context of the current clashes, the term "martyr" is applied to all individuals killed, wounded, or imprisoned in events related to what has become known as the "al-Aqsa intifada," including those who carried out suicide attacks. The term "martyr" is even applied as an honorific to some prominent individuals who, since September 2000, died of natural causes.[83]

In Palestinian Arabic, the phrase for a bombing attack in which the perpetrator is killed is an *amaliyya istishhadiyya,* a "martyrdom operation," or an *amaliyya fida'iyya,* a "sacrificial operation." In the Israeli Arabic-language media, the preferred term is an *amaliyya intihariyya,* a "suicide operation."[84]

The media coverage comprises only part of a larger atmosphere of social respect for those who have died in the intifada, expressed through street posters, pamphlets, internet sites, murals, banners, public discourse, and attendance by public officials at funerals or memorial ceremonies. Virtually all societies engaged in armed struggle honor those who die as part of the struggle. What is wrong, however, is to equate individuals who are victims of attacks or who have carried out attacks that are permissible under international humanitarian law with individuals who die while committing war crimes or crimes against humanity.

Public officials, because of the political authority they embody, should never legitimize attacks on civilians. Yet political leaders have made statements that appear to endorse attacks against civilians, both within the Occupied Territories and externally. These span the range from ambiguity to outright

---

[83] For example, the late Palestine Liberation Organization representative, Faisal Husseini, for whom posters were prominently displayed in East Jerusalem in 2001-2002.

[84] Arabic-language media in other countries have used varying terms. See, for example, Daniel Sobelman, "Saudi Media Drops Shaheed in Coverage of Suicide Attacks," *Ha'aretz,* May 22, 2002.

support, and undermine other statements condemning attacks against civilians.[85] Political leaders such as President Arafat have repeatedly praised "martyrs," without distinguishing between those who die as victims of attacks or while attacking military targets and those who intentionally die in the course of a deliberate attack against civilians.[86] Yasir Abed Rabbo, the PA minister of culture and information, reportedly defended the use of the term "martyr" with reference to suicide bombers. "You can call him a *shahid* and denounce what he does politically," he said.[87]

Other officials have expressed more unequivocal support for attacks on civilians. On April 10, 2002, PA Cabinet Secretary-General Ahmad 'Abd al-Rahman described that day's attack on a Haifa bus as a "natural response to what is taking place in Palestinian camps."[88] Six weeks later, 'Abd al-Rahman described suicide bombings in an interview with the Qatar-based satellite television station al-Jazeera as "the highest form of national struggle. There is no argument about that."[89] Other officials have praised the armed groups that perpetrate the attacks, rather than the attacks themselves. In March 2002, after repeated al-Aqsa Martyrs' Brigades attacks on civilians, West Bank Preventive Security chief Jibril Rajoub reportedly told a local newspaper, "The Aqsa Brigades are the noblest phenomenon in the history of Fatah, because they restored the movement's honor and bolstered the political and security echelon of the Palestinian Authority."[90]

Statements approving of suicide attacks have also been made by government officials of neighboring countries. On March 27, the day of the

---

[85] See for example, "Statement in the name of Mr. President and Palestinian Leadership: Condemning all terrorist acts targeting civilians, be they Israelis or Palestinians, including state, group or individuals terrorism," April 13, 2002 at http://www.jmcc.org/banner/banner1/bayan/pasterror.htm (accessed September 3, 2002).

[86] See for example, interviews by Arafat with Abu Dhabi Television on March 29, 2002, re-broadcast by PA TV the same day. See transcript of the interview in "Palestinian leader says "morale is high" among followers in compound," BBC Monitoring Middle East, March 29, 2002.

[87] "The cancer of suicide bombing," *New York Times*, April 3, 2002.

[88] See report by Palestinian Satellite Channel TV Gaza in "Palestinian official says suicide bomb "natural response" to Israeli offensive," BBC Monitoring Middle East, April 10, 2002.

[89] See transcript of interview with al-Jazeera in Jerusalem Media and Communication Centre Daily Report, May 13, 2001.

[90] Arieh O'Sullivan and Lamia Lahoud, "Rajoub praises Aksa Martyrs' Brigades," *Jerusalem Post*, March 19, 2002.

bombing of the Park Hotel, Syrian President Bashar al-Asad said in a speech to the Arab Summit in Beirut:

> We have heard today in a speech by one of the guests on the doctrine governing attacks on civilians and the innocent.... The doctrine governing attacks on civilians and the innocent is a correct one ...but it is not applicable in this situation. We are now facing occupation. Attacking civilians when there are two neighboring states that are involved in military operations is one thing, but when there is occupation it is a different issue.[91]

In a June 2002 interview with the London-based Arabic newspaper, *al-Sharq al-Awsat,* the Saudi ambassador to the U.K said, "I wish I would die a martyr despite the fact that I am of an age that does not allow me to carry out a martyrdom operation."[92] Such comments glorify individuals who die in order to attack civilians. They contribute to public acceptance of such attacks, and, in the context of ongoing suicide attacks against civilians, publicly legitimize war crimes or crimes against humanity. Public officials have a responsibility not to make such statements—and to discourage others from making them.

Apologetic statements by public officials have also been accompanied by the broadcast of incendiary statements on publicly funded television. There were several recorded instances of such broadcasts on the official PA television channel in 2001, particularly in the broadcasts of weekly Friday prayer sermons. Among these were the live broadcasts of Shaikh Ibrahim Ma`adi delivering sermons from a Gaza mosque on June 8, 2001, and again on August 3, 2001. "Blessed are the people who strap bombs onto their bodies or those of their sons," Ma'adi said on the first of these occasions. On the second, he explicitly called for bombings in Tel Aviv, Hadera, Ashkelon, and other Israeli cities, adding:

---

[91] Speech by His Excellency the President Bashar al-Asad in the Opening Session of the Fourteenth   Arab   Summit,   March   27,   2002,   Beirut   at http://www.arabsummitbeirut.org/submenu2c_a_syriacomplete.htm (accessed June 5, 2002). Ellipses in original text. Translated from Arabic by Human Rights Watch.

[92] Interview by Huda al-Husayni with Ghazi al-Qusaybi, Saudi Ambassador to the United Kingdom, *al-Sharq al-Awsat,* 5 June 2002, pp. 8-9. FBIS Daily Report, FBIS-NES-2002-0605. In September 2002, Ambassador al-Qusaybi was recalled from his post. There was no indication from Saudi authorities if his well-publicized endorsements of suicide bombings were a factor.

The Jews have bared their teeth. They have said what they have said and done what they have done. And they will not be deterred except by the color of the blood of their filthy people. They will not be deterred unless we willingly and voluntarily blow ourselves up among them.[93]

In the context of the Israeli-Palestinian conflict, such statements constitute incitement to crimes against humanity. Under international criminal law, the PA has a responsibility to ensure they are neither broadcast nor published, and should bring to justice those who make them. The PA is also obliged to prevent such incitement under article XII (1) of the 1994 Gaza-Jericho Agreement and Article II (3) (c) of Annex I to the Israel-Palestinian Interm Agreement on the West Bank and the Gaza Strip.[94] These Friday sermons are broadcast live, usually from a prominent mosque in Gaza or the West Bank, implying that the broadcaster has limited control over the message. However, the PA has a responsibility to ensure that individuals speaking on live broadcasts are aware that they will be held criminally liable if they incite the commission of crimes against humanity or war crimes. Those who contravene such warnings should be held accountable and brought to justice.

Hani al-Masri, an official in the PA Ministry of Information and outspoken critic of suicide bombing attacks on civilians, told Human Rights Watch that PA television programming policies have changed since December 2001. "There is more coverage [of suicide bombings] on CNN than on Palestinian TV," Masri said.[95]

Journalists used to be more supportive of the suicide bombings, reflecting public opinion, but now they have come out more clearly against them. The editors determine what gets broadcast, and they reflect the line of the PA. Before December 16 [2001] the message was a mixed one. The PA now seems to be trying hard through TV. The dominant sound bite is that armed resistance is for the Occupied

---

[93] Copy of broadcasts provided to Human Rights Watch by Itamar Marcus of the Israel-based Palestinian Media Watch

[94] *Agreement On The Gaza Strip And The Jericho Area*, between the State of Israel and the PLO, May 4, 1994, Article XII (1); Annex I, "Protocol Concerning Redeployment and Security Arrangements, The Israeli-Palestinian Interim Agreement on the West Bank and the Gaza Strip," Washington D.C., September 28, 1995, Article II (3) (c).

[95] Human Rights Watch telephone interview with Hani al-Masri, Ramallah, June 19, 2002.

Territories only, against the occupation forces. But people here are extremely disenchanted with the PA after Oslo, after the Israeli reoccupation. And the PA has no say in the mosques, which are much more important than the media.... We can't say there's been a media campaign against these attacks, but debates and critical discussions are more frequent.[96]

Ziad Abu `Amr, a Palestinian legislator in Gaza and prominent critic of PA policies, agreed with Masri:

The debate about suicide bombers is growing, but it's still largely overwhelmed by the desperateness of our situation. The problem is that few people here watch Palestine TV. They watch Jazeera and Manar. You want to see incitement? That's where it is.[97]

Systematic monitoring required to evaluate such assessments of Palestinian media is beyond the scope of Human Rights Watch's research. Ghassan Khatib, founder and director of the Jerusalem Media and Communications Center, also argued that the prime sources of media encouragement for suicide bombings are not under the control of the PA. "Look at the media—it's a free platform for Hamas," he said, speaking of Gulf states' support for Hamas. "Jazeera has not been at all professional in the way it favors Hamas over other factions, and promotes anything that's critical of the PA and PLO [Palestine Liberation Organization]."[98]

Palestinian public debate over suicide attacks against civilians has grown since March 2002. For example, on June 19, 2002, in a full-page advertisement in the Palestinian daily *al-Quds*, fifty-five public personalities and intellectuals published an "Urgent Appeal to Stop Suicide Bombings." Sari Nusseibeh, the president of al-Quds University and the PLO representative for Jerusalem, reportedly organized the initiative that Palestinian newspapers both welcomed and criticized. The following day, President Arafat welcomed the petition in an interview with *Ha'aretz*, and repeated his condemnation of attacks on

---

[96] Ibid.

[97] Human Rights Watch interview with Ziad Abu `Amr, Washington, D.C., June 28, 2002.

[98] Human Rights Watch interview with Ghassan Khatib, Jerusalem, June 6, 2002. Khatib was subsequently appointed minister of labor in the PA cabinet.

civilians.[99] More than four hundred additional signatures were gathered in subsequent days, triggering criticism from Hamas and a counter-petition in support of "all means" of armed struggle, supported by some one hundred and fifty signatures.[100] Some PA officials subsequently spoke out more strongly against suicide bombings. On August 30, PA Interior Minister `Abd al-Razaq Yahya gave a widely-publicized interview with the Israeli newspaper *Yediot Ahronoth*, in which he urged all armed groups to stop suicide attacks because they were "contrary to the Palestinian tradition, against international law and harm[ed] the Palestinian people."[101]

---

[99] See Akiva Eldar, "Arafat to Ha'aretz: I Accept Clinton's Proposal to Bring Order," *Ha'aretz*, June 21, 2002. Translated from Hebrew by Human Rights Watch. See text of statement from WAFA (official PA news agency) in "Arafat Receives Chinese Official, Condemns Violence Against Civilians," BBC Monitoring Middle East, June 20, 2002.

[100] For an English translation of the text and some critical responses from Palestinian political figures, including Hamas' `Abd al-`Aziz al-Rantisi, see Middle East Media Research Institute, "Special dispatch no. 393, A Palestinian Communiqué Against Martyrdom Attacks," June 25, 2002 at http://www.memri.org (accessed August 29, 2002). See also James Bennet, "Gingerly, Arabs Question Suicide Bombings," *New York Times*, July 3, 2002.

[101] See Mark Lavie, "Palestinian: Stop Suicide Bombings," Associated Press, August 30, 2002.

IV. LEGAL STANDARDS

In any armed conflict the right of the parties to choose the methods and means of warfare is not unlimited. On the contrary, those choices are strictly regulated by the customs and provisions of the law of armed conflict, referred to here as international humanitarian law (IHL). [102] IHL also regulates cases of total or partial military occupation, as in the case of the Palestinian territories. Against this background, certain episodes of violence that rise to the level of armed conflict are governed by general principles of the laws of war. Some of the rules of IHL form part of international customary law, which are binding on all states and also on non-state actors—in this case, Palestinian armed groups. [103]

Many rules of IHL have been codified in international treaties, such as the Geneva Conventions and their additional protocols. The Geneva Conventions have achieved widespread acceptance among states as authoritative standards of behavior for parties in situations of armed conflict, and have been ratified by more than 190 states. [104] The 1977 Additional Protocols to the Geneva Conventions were negotiated at a diplomatic conference where representatives from non-state armed groups campaigning for national self-determination were also present, including the Palestine Liberation Organization (PLO). [105] Many of the provisions are recognized as customary international law.

---

[102] Article 2, paragraph 2, common to the four Geneva Conventions of August 12, 1949. The Geneva Conventions of August 12, 1949; the Protocols Additional to the Geneva Conventions of June 8, 1977; and their commentaries are available at http://www.icrc.org/ihl (accessed September 3, 2002).

[103] A rule is customary if it reflects state practice and there exists a conviction in the international community that such practice is required as a matter of law. While treaties only bind those states that have ratified them, customary law binds all states. See International Committee of the Red Cross (ICRC), "Treaties and Customary Law" at http://www.icrc.org/Web/eng/siteeng0.nsf/iwpList2/Humanitarian_law:Treaties_and_cust omary_law (accessed September 3, 2002). For a discussion on customary law binding individuals and non-state actors, see Lindsay Moir, *The Law of Internal Armed Conflict* (United Kingdom: Cambridge University Press, 2002), pp. 57-58; and Rene Provost, *International Human Rights and Humanitarian Law* (United Kingdom: Cambridge University Press, 2002), pp. 98-99.

[104] Including Algeria, Bahrain, Iran, Iraq, Israel, Egypt, Jordan, Kuwait, Lebanon, Libya, Morocco, Oman, Qatar, Sudan, Saudi Arabia, Syria, Tunisia, Turkey, the United Arab Emirates, and Yemen.

[105] The non-state participants in the meeting, which also included the African National Congress, did not vote.

Obligations of the Palestinian Authority and Armed Palestinian Groups

The rules and obligations of IHL are clearest when applied to conflict between sovereign states. The responsibilities of non-state actors may differ from those of sovereign states, but non-state actors, too, have clear responsibilities under IHL. Many customary rules of IHL apply to all parties to a conflict, including non-state actors, provided that the confrontation is of an intensity that places it beyond the threshold of a mere disturbance.[106]

Although it is not a sovereign state, the Palestinian Authority has explicit security and legal obligations set out in the Oslo Accords, an umbrella term for the series of agreements negotiated between the government of Israel and the PLO from 1993 to 1996. The PA obligations to maintain security and public order were set out in articles XII to XV of the 1995 Interim Agreement on the West Bank and Gaza Strip.[107] These responsibilities were elaborated further in Annex I of the interim agreement, which specifies that the PA will bring to justice those accused of perpetrating attacks against Israeli civilians. According to article II (3) (c) of the annex, the PA will "apprehend, investigate and prosecute perpetrators and all other persons directly or indirectly involved in acts of terrorism, violence and incitement."[108]

Similarly, PA leaders, including President Arafat, have repeatedly pledged in meetings with international human rights organizations and in radio broadcasts, as well as in the Oslo Accords, that the PA intends to abide by internationally recognized human rights norms.[109] In a situation of clashes that

---

[106] Article 3 common to the four Geneva Conventions of August 12, 1949 (Common Article 3), accepted as customary law, has wide scope. The authoritative commentary of the ICRC to the Fourth Geneva Convention justifies applying the provision to non-state actors, saying "[t]here can be no drawbacks in this, since the Article in its reduced form, contrary to what might be thought, does not in any way limit the right of a State to put down rebellion, nor does it increase in the slightest the authority of the rebel party. It merely demands respect for certain rules, which were already recognized as essential in all civilized countries, and embodied in the municipal law of the States in question, long before the Convention was signed." ICRC, "Commentary: Convention (IV) relative to the Protection of Civilian Persons in Time of War. Geneva, 12 August 1949" at http://www.icrc.org/ihl (accessed September 3, 2002).

[107] The Government of Israel and the Palestine Liberation Organization, "The Israeli-Palestinian Interim Agreement on the West Bank and the Gaza Strip," Washington D.C., September 28, 1995.

[108] See article II (3) (c) in Annex I, "Protocol Concerning Redeployment and Security Arrangements, The Israeli-Palestinian Interim Agreement on the West Bank and the Gaza Strip," Washington D.C., September 28, 1995.

[109] Under article XI (1) of Annex I, "Protocol Concerning Redeployment. . ." of the interim agreement of September 28, 1995, the Palestinian Police "will exercise powers and responsibilities to implement this Memorandum with due regard to internationally

rise to the level of armed conflict, PA security forces and other organized factions that engage in armed actions should abide by fundamental principles of international humanitarian law. They are also obliged to ensure respect for such principles by armed groups operating from territory under their effective control.

The Palestinian Authority exists independently from the Palestine Liberation Organization. From 1974 to 1977, the PLO was one of several national liberation movements "recognized by the regional intergovernmental organizations" to participate in the diplomatic negotiations on the text of the two Additional Protocols to the Geneva Conventions.[110] Under article 96 of Protocol I, non-state actors may commit, under certain specific circumstances, to apply the conventions and the protocol if they declare their willingness to do so to the Swiss government. The PLO has never made a declaration under article 96, and Israel is not a party to Protocol I. As a result, Protocol I does not apply to the current clashes, except for the provisions of Protocol I that are considered customary international law.

The PLO Executive Committee wrote to the Swiss Federal Department of Foreign Affairs in June 1989 to inform it that, being "entrusted with the functions of the Government of the State of Palestine by decision of the Palestinian National Council," it had decided on May 4, 1989 to adhere to the Geneva Conventions and their additional protocols.[111] Due to the "uncertainty within the international community as to the existence or non-existence of a State of Palestine," the Swiss government informed states that it could not decide whether the PLO letter constituted a valid instrument of accession. As a result of their unilateral declaration, the PLO and its constituent factions have nevertheless undertaken what is, at minimum, a strong moral commitment to uphold the most fundamental standards contained in the Geneva Conventions and Protocol I.

Crimes Against Humanity

The scale and systematic nature of the attacks on civilians detailed in this report meets the definition of a crime against humanity. Hamas and Islamic Jihad have claimed responsibility for suicide bombing attacks on civilians since

---

accepted norms of human rights and the rule of law, and will be guided by the need to protect the public, respect human dignity, and avoid harassment."

[110] *Final Act of the Diplomatic Conference of Geneva of 1974-1977,* Geneva, June 10, 1977.

[111] ICRC, "Geneva Conventions of 12 August 1949 and Additional Protocols of 8 June 1977: Ratifications, accessions and successions" at http://www.icrc.org/Web/Eng/siteeng0.nsf/iwpList74/77EA1BDEE20B4CCDC1256B66 00595596#a6 (accessed September 3, 2002).

1994, and such attacks clearly represent organizational policy at the highest levels. Since January 2002, the al-Aqsa Martyrs' Brigades and the PFLP have also claimed responsibility for organizing and carrying out such attacks.

The notion of "crimes against humanity" refers to acts that, by their scale or nature, outrage the conscience of humankind. Crimes against humanity were first codified in the charter of the Nuremberg Tribunal of 1945. Since then, the concept has been incorporated into a number of international treaties, including the Rome Statute of the International Criminal Court (ICC). Although definitions of crimes against humanity differ slightly from treaty to treaty, all definitions provide that the deliberate, widespread, or systematic killing of civilians by an organization or government is a crime against humanity.[112] Unlike war crimes, crimes against humanity may be committed in times of peace or in periods of unrest that do not rise to the level of an armed conflict.

The most recent definition of crimes against humanity is contained in the Rome Statute of the ICC, which entered into force on July 1, 2002. The statute defines crimes against humanity as the "participation in and knowledge of a widespread or systematic attack against a civilian population," and "the multiple commission of [such] acts…against any civilian population, pursuant to or in furtherance of a State or organizational policy to commit such attack." The statute's introduction defines "policy to commit such attack" to mean that the state or organization actively promoted or encouraged such attacks against a civilian population. The elements of the "crime against humanity of murder" require that (1) "the perpetrator killed one or more persons," (2) "[t]he conduct was committed as part of a widespread or systematic attack directed against a civilian population," and (3) "[t]he perpetrator knew that the conduct was part

---

[112] One example of a definition is contained in article 18 of the Draft Code of Crimes Against the Peace and Security of Mankind, drafted by the expert members of the International Law Commission. Article 18 uses a definition of crimes against humanity based on the Nuremberg Charter, but also takes into account developments in international law since Nuremberg. It sets out two conditions that must be met for acts such as murder, enslavement, mutilation, and rape to qualify as crimes against humanity. The first was that the act be committed "in a systematic manner or on a large scale," meaning that it must have been committed as a result of a deliberate plan or policy, usually resulting in repeated acts. The second condition was that the acts be directed against multiple victims, either "as a result of the cumulative effect of a series of inhumane acts or the singular effect of an inhumane act of extraordinary magnitude." See "Article 18—Crimes Against Humanity" in chapter II, "Draft Code of Crimes Against the Peace and Security of Mankind" in the *International Law Commission Report*, 1996 at http://www.un.org/law/ilc/reports/1996/chap02.htm#doc3 (accessed September 3, 2002).

of, or intended the conduct to be part of, a widespread or systematic attack against a civilian population."[113]

Those who commit crimes against humanity, like war crimes, are held individually criminally responsible for their actions. Crimes against humanity give rise to universal jurisdiction, they do not admit the defense of following superior orders, and they do not benefit from statutes of limitation. International jurisprudence and standard setting of the last ten years have consolidated the view that those responsible for crimes against humanity and other serious violations of human rights should not be granted amnesty.[114] As in the case of war crimes, all states are responsible for bringing those who commit crimes against humanity to justice.

The pattern of suicide bombing attacks against Israel civilians that emerged in 2001 and intensified during 2002 clearly meets the criteria of a crime against humanity.

War Crimes: The Prohibition Against Targeting Civilians

A fundamental rule of international humanitarian law is that civilians must enjoy general protection against danger arising from military operations. The rule of civilian immunity is one of "the oldest fundamental maxims" of international customary law, meaning that it is binding on all parties to a conflict, regardless of whether a conflict is international or non-international in character.[115] Non-state parties to a conflict are also obliged to respect the norms of customary international law. At all times, it is forbidden to direct attacks

---

[113] Article 7(1)(a), "Finalized draft text of the Elements of Crimes Adopted by the Preparatory Commission for the International Criminal Court," November 2, 2000, U.N. Document PCNICC/2000/1/Add.2.

[114] For example, on July 7, 1999, the Special Representative of the Secretary-General attached a disclaimer to the Sierra Leone Peace Agreement, saying "The United Nations interprets that the amnesty and pardon in article nine of this agreement shall not apply to international crimes of genocide, crimes against humanity, war crimes, and other serious violations of international humanitarian law." See also, Commission on Human Rights, resolutions 1999/34 and 1999/32; the Annual Report of the U.N. Committee Against Torture to the General Assembly, 09/07/1996,A/51/44, para. 117; and U.N. Human Rights Committee General Comment 20, April 10, 1992.

[115] Dieter Fleck (ed.), *The Handbook of Humanitarian Law in Armed Conflict* (Oxford: Oxford University Press, 1995), p. 120. "The general prohibition against indiscriminate warfare applies independently of Arts. 48 and 51 [of Protocol I]. The relevant provisions of the Additional Protocols merely codify pre-existing customary law, because the principle of distinction belongs to the oldest fundamental maxims of established customary rules of humanitarian law. It is also virtually impossible to distinguish between international and non-international armed conflicts in this respect."

against civilians; indeed, to attack civilians intentionally while aware of their civilian status is a war crime. It is thus an imperative duty for an attacker to identify and distinguish non-combatants from combatants in every situation.

In addition to its status as established customary law, the principle of civilian immunity has been codified in numerous treaties. One of the clearest expressions of the principle is set out in article 51(2) of Additional Protocol I to the Geneva Conventions, which states:

> The civilian population as such, as well as individual civilians, shall not be the object of attack. Acts or threats of violence, the primary purpose of which is to spread terror among the civilian population, are prohibited.[116]

By deliberately targeting civilians, suicide bombing attacks clearly violate this most fundamental rule of the laws of war. The prohibition against targeting civilians holds in all circumstances, including when a party undertakes such attacks in retaliation for attacks on its own civilians (discussed below).[117]

The principle of distinction between civilian and military targets is enshrined in article 48 of Protocol I:

> In order to ensure respect for and protection of the civilian population and civilian objects, the Parties to the conflict shall at all times distinguish between the civilian population and combatants, and between civilian objects and military objectives, and accordingly shall direct their operations only against military objectives.[118]

Military objectives are defined as "those objects, which by their nature, location, purpose or use make an effective contribution to military action."[119] Under international humanitarian law, attacks that are not, or as a result of the method of attack *cannot,* be aimed at military targets, are considered "indiscriminate." They are prohibited under Protocol I and, under the same treaty, constitute war

---

[116] Protocol Additional to the Geneva Conventions of August 12, 1949, and relating to the Protection of Victims of International Armed Conflicts (Protocol I), June 8, 1977 at http://www.unhchr.ch/html/menu3/b/93.htm (accessed October 8, 2002).

[117] Protocol I, Art. 51(6).

[118] Protocol I, Art. 48.

[119] Protocol I, Art. 52(2).

crimes.[120] The protocol's provisions prohibiting indiscriminate warfare are considered to be norms of customary international law, binding on all parties in a conflict, regardless of whether it is an international or internal armed conflict.[121] That is, they are binding on all parties to the Israeli-Palestinian conflict, even though Israel has not ratified Protocol I.

Murder and Willful Killings

In all situations of armed conflict, the deliberate killing of civilians is a war crime. Common Article 3 of the 1949 Geneva Conventions prohibits "violence to life and person, in particular murder of all kinds, mutilation, cruel treatment, and torture" when perpetrated against persons "taking no active part in the hostilities." As noted, Israel has ratified the 1949 Geneva Conventions. The obligation contained in Common Article 3 is absolute. It applies regardless of whether a party to the conflict is a state.[122] Serious violations of Common Article 3 are increasingly considered to be war crimes, and have been defined as such in the statutes of the International Criminal Court, the International Criminal Tribunal for the former Yugoslavia (ICTY), and the International Criminal Tribunal for Rwanda.[123]

Willful killing, that is, *intentionally* causing the death of civilians, and "willfully causing great suffering or serious injury" when wounding victims, are

---

[120] Indiscriminate attacks are "those which are not directed against a military objective," "those which employ a method or means of combat which cannot be directed at a specific military objective," or "those which employ a method or means of combat, the effects of which cannot be limited as required by the Protocol," and "consequently, in each such case, are of a nature to strike military objectives and civilians or civilian objects without distinction." Definitions of war crimes under Protocol I are contained in article 85.

[121] Fleck (Ed.), *The Handbook of Humanitarian Law,* p. 120.

[122] The ICRC commentary notes that the term "each Party" also binds a "non-signatory Party—a Party, moreover, which was not yet in existence [at the time of the Diplomatic Conference] and which need not even represent a legal entity capable of undertaking international obligations." The commentary continues, "[t]he obligation is absolute for each of the Parties." It further states: "If an insurgent party applies Article 3, so much the better for the victims of the conflict. No one will complain. If it does not apply it, it will prove that those who regard its actions as mere acts of anarchy or brigandage are right." ICRC, Commentary to the Fourth Geneva Convention at http://www.icrc.org/ihl (accessed September 3, 2002).

[123] S.R. Ratner, "Categories of War Crimes" in Roy Gutman and David Rieff (eds.), *Crimes of War,* (New York: W.W. Norton and Co., 1999).

war crimes.[124]   Persons who commit, order, or condone war crimes are individually liable under international humanitarian law for their crimes.

Justifications Offered by Palestinian Armed Groups

Representatives of armed Palestinian groups often acknowledge they are aware that suicide attacks against civilians breach fundamental norms of international humanitarian law. However, they frequently invoke several arguments in an attempt to justify suicide attacks. The first argument is that such attacks do not target civilians. The second is that international humanitarian law does not regulate the conduct of Palestinian armed groups. The third is that those targeted in the suicide bombing attacks are some how not entitled to civilian status. The fourth is that suicide bombing attacks on civilians are legitimate because there is no other way to compensate for the imbalance of means between armed Palestinian groups and the Israeli security forces. None of these arguments has merit.

Despite overwhelming evidence to the contrary, members of armed Palestinian groups frequently deny that their operations target civilians. When a founding member of the al-Aqsa Martyrs' Brigades, Mahmud al-Titi, was interviewed on March 8, 2002 about a shooting attack at a Tel Aviv restaurant three days earlier, al-Titi maintained—without much apparent conviction—that he had instructed the perpetrator to target soldiers or police. "I believe he saw soldiers or guards next to the restaurant or maybe he didn't find soldiers or police and so attacked the closest target."[125] Shortly before he was assassinated on May 22, 2002, al-Titi publicly tried to distance himself from the al-Aqsa Martyrs' Brigades' string of civilian attacks: "I want to fight whoever is in charge of the government of Israel, not civilians," he said. "We were delivering the wrong message to the world."[126]

---

[124] Those violations of international humanitarian law that are "grave breaches" of the Fourth Geneva Convention are enumerated in article 147, and include willful killing, torture or inhuman treatment, and "willfully causing great suffering or serious injury to body or health." These violations, including acts of willful killing, are also specified as war crimes under article 8 of the Rome Statute establishing the International Criminal Court, which has jurisdiction over these crimes after July 1, 2002 for states that have ratified the statute, or in situations in which the U.N. Security Council refers the conduct to the ICC for prosecution.

[125] Mohammed Daraghmeh, "Militia leader seeks to build Palestinian liberation arm," Associated Press, March 8, 2002.

[126] C.J. Chivers, "Palestinian militant group says it will limit bombings," *New York Times,* April 23, 2002. In this interview, al-Titi used his *nom de guerre*, Abu Mujahid. He was identified by his real name in an interview published several days later. Mohammad Bazzi, "Out of hiding for interview, al-Aqsa leader is defiant," *Newsday,* April 25, 2002.

Since October 2000, Hamas has carried out eighteen suicide attacks against civilians, more than any other group. In an on-line interview, Salah Shehadah, the leader of the Hamas military wing, was asked: "There are allegations against Hamas that it targets civilians through martyrdom operations, what's your take on that?" Shehadah responded, implicitly conceding that some categories of civilians were targeted: `

> Our stand is not to target children, the elderly, or places of prayer—even though these places of prayer incite the killing of Muslims. Up until now we have not targeted schools ...nor do we target hospitals, even though they are an easy target. That is because we are working in accordance with certain values ...we don't fight Jews because they are Jewish but because they occupy our lands. So if children are killed it is something outside of our hands.[127]

Wars Against Alien Occupation or in Exercise of the Right of Self-Determination

Palestinian groups and spokespersons have claimed that the practice of targeting civilians is somehow exempt from condemnation as a war crime or crime against humanity because of the exceptional character of their struggle for "national liberation." A typical example is a statement by Hassan Salameh, a Hamas member from Gaza now imprisoned for life for his role in the 1996 suicide bombings: "I am not a murderer.... Even if civilians are killed, it's not because we like it or are bloodthirsty. It is a fact of life in a people's struggle against a foreign occupier. A suicide bombing is the highest level of jihad and highlights the depth of our faith."[128]

However, article 1(4) of Additional Protocol I, which was expressly intended to cover wars of national liberation, states that the Protocol and all its principles and provisions cover "armed conflicts in which people are fighting against colonial domination and alien occupation and against racist regimes in the exercise of their right of self-determination...."[129] As mentioned, the PLO,

---

Al-Titi and two fellow al-Aqsa Martyrs' Brigades militants were assassinated on May 22, 2002.

[127] Anonymous article entitled, "Head of the military wing of Hamas discloses for the first time secrets of martyrs, their operations and their weapons," posted on `Izz al-Din al-Qasasm website, www.qassam.net/chat/salah3.html (in Arabic) (accessed August 8, 2002). Translated by Human Rights Watch.

[128] Jerrold M. Post and Ehud Sprinzak, "Terror's Aftermath: A convicted Hamas terrorist talks about his mission to destroy Israel," *Los Angeles Times*, July 7, 2002.

[129] Protocol I, Art. 1(4).

as the recognized representative of the Palestinian people, participated in the negotiation of Additional Protocol I from 1974 to 1977. Israel has not ratified Protocol I, and this particular provision is not considered customary international law. However, given the wide extent of the ratification of Protocol I, article 1(4) represents a significant trend in establishing that the fundamental rules of international humanitarian law apply even in wars of national liberation.[130]

The language of Protocol I expressly prohibits attacks against civilians, as discussed above. Article 51(2) of Additional Protocol I states unambiguously that "[t]he civilian population as such, as well as individual civilians, shall not be the object of attack. Acts or threats of violence, the primary purpose of which is to spread terror among the civilian population, are prohibited."[131]

Retaliation and Reprisals

Palestinian groups responsible for suicide bombing attacks against civilians have commonly claimed that such attacks are legitimate because they are carried out in retaliation for real or perceived Israeli violations of international humanitarian law. For example, Hamas leader Ismail Abu Shanab told Human Rights Watch:

> It's not targeting civilians. It is saying that if you attack mine I'll attack yours. If we say yes, we'll stop—can the world guarantee Israel will stop? The rules of the game were set by the other side. If you follow all our martyrdom operations, you will find that they all came after their massacres. We would accept the rules [of international humanitarian law] if Israel would use them. If you ask us to comply, that is not difficult. Islamic teachings support the Geneva Conventions. They are accepted. When it comes to the other party, if they don't abide, we cannot be obliged to them, except insofar as we can achieve something."[132]

Islamic Jihad and Fatah leaders have made similar statements. But this argument is both incorrect and, insofar as others are encouraged to act according to this view, damaging.

---

[130] As of September 1, 2002, 159 states had become parties to Additional Protocol I.

[131] Protocol I, Art. 51(2).

[132] Human Rights Watch interview with Ismail Abu Shanab, Gaza City, May 15, 2002.

The idea that suicide attacks against Israeli civilians are legitimate retaliation for Israeli attacks has had great resonance with Palestinian public opinion. Public opinion polls indicate that the overwhelming majority of Palestinians, including many who are opposed to attacks against civilians, also oppose PA arrests of members of the perpetrator groups.[133] One Palestinian academic told Human Rights Watch: "None of us want to do these things. It is imposed on us. We know about the Geneva Conventions, the need to distinguish, but what we see on the ground is something different."[134]

Under international humanitarian law, a failure by one party to a conflict to respect the laws of war does not relieve the other of its obligation to respect those laws. That obligation is absolute, not premised on reciprocity.

The Geneva Conventions specifically *prohibit* reprisals against civilians, private property of civilians in occupied territory, or enemy foreigners on friendly territory.[135] Additional Protocol I is similarly unambiguous on reprisals: "Attacks against the civilian population or civilians by way of reprisals are prohibited."[136] Although the relevant provision of Protocol I has not yet reached the status of customary law, it expresses the prevailing trend in IHL to prohibit reprisal attacks against civilians—and thereby pre-empt the vicious spirals of reprisal and counter-reprisal that frequently follow.[137]

---

[133] In a survey by the Palestinian Center for Policy and Survey Research (PSR), 86 percent of respondents opposed the arrest of individuals who had carried out attacks inside Israel. PSR Public Opinion Poll no. 4, May 15-19, 2002 at http://www.pcpsr.org/survey/polls/2002/p4a.html (accessed September 3, 2002).

[134] Human Rights Watch interview, name withheld, Jenin, June 10, 2002.

[135] Fourth Geneva Convention, Art. 33(3).

[136] Protocol I, Art. 51(6). According to the ICRC commentary, "This provision is very important," noting that the belligerents in World War II, after declaring publicly that attacks are only permissible against military objects, subsequently "on the pretext that their own population had been hit by attacks carried out by the adversary, they went so far, by way of reprisals, as to wage war almost indiscriminately, and this resulted in countless civilian victims." ICRC, "Commentary to Protocol Additional to the Geneva Conventions of 12 August 1949, and relating to the Protection of Victims of International Armed Conflicts (Protocol I), 8 June 1977" at http://www.icrc.org/ihl (accessed September 3, 2002).

[137] See generally, T. Meron, "The Humanization of Humanitarian Law," 94 *American Journal of International Law*, 239, 249-251. Israel could help dispel any doubt about the applicability of the rule against reprisals by ratifying Protocol I.

Who is a Civilian?

Another justification put forward by the perpetrators of attacks against civilians is that the individuals targeted are somehow not entitled to civilian status. As discussed earlier, the distinction between civilians and combatants is fundamental to the protections of international humanitarian law.

Under IHL, anyone who is not a combatant is considered a civilian.[138] Reserve or off-duty soldiers are considered civilians unless they take part directly in hostilities, or become subject to military command. Civilians lose their civilian protection if they directly participate in armed hostilities, but only during the period of that participation; they regain civilian status once they are no longer directly engaged in hostilities.

Civilian Residents of Illegal Settlements as "Legitimate Targets"

Palestinian armed groups that have targeted Israeli civilians argue that Israeli settlers in the Occupied Territories have forfeited their civilian status because they reside in settlements that are illegal under international humanitarian law.[139] Leaders of Hamas and Islamic Jihad, the groups that pioneered the use of suicide bomb attacks against civilians, have further stated that they consider all of Israel to be "occupied territory," all Jewish Israelis to be settlers, and thus all Israelis to be legitimate targets.

This position is exemplified by statements such as those of Hamas's leader, Shaikh Ahmad Yassin. In August 2001, in the aftermath of the suicide bombing attack on the Sbarro pizzeria, Yassin said, "The Geneva Convention protects civilians in occupied territories, not civilians who are in fact occupiers. All of

---

[138] Under article 50(1) of Protocol I a civilian is defined as someone who is not a member of any organized armed forces of a party to a conflict. The same article adds that "[i]n cases of doubt whether a person is a civilian, that person shall be considered to be a civilian." Under article 51(3), civilians that directly participate in hostilities lose civilian protection for the duration of such participation.

[139] Article 49(6) of the Fourth Geneva Convention states that "[t]he Occupying Power shall not deport or transfer parts of its own civilian population into the territory it occupies." Successive Israeli governments have given active support to the settlement policy since 1967, inconsistent with the aims of the Fourth Geneva Convention, which was intended to protect the civilian population of occupied territories from 'colonization' and other similar policies detrimental to their well being. See ICRC Commentary to the Fourth Geneva Convention at http://www.icrc.org/ihl (accessed September 3, 2002). Civilian settlements also violate the prohibition on creating permanent changes in the occupied territories that are not for the benefit of the occupied population ("protected persons"), as reflected in article 55 of the 1907 Hague Regulations.

Israel, Tel Aviv included, is occupied Palestine. So we're not actually targeting civilians—that would go against Islam."[140]

Even Palestinians who criticize attacks against civilians frequently excuse attacks against settlers. The fact that many individual settlers carry arms, arguably for their own defense, appears to have given a new argument to armed groups to justify attacks against civilians. "They are not civilians," Islamic Jihad spokesperson Ismail Abu Shanab told Human Rights Watch.

> Not because the settlements are not legal but because the settlers are militias. They are not civilians. They have guns and are armed. Every home and settler has a gun, and all these people are militants and targets. They can't hide in the uniform of a civilian.... If I see women and children I must not shoot. We can't behave without humanity. But in principle, settlers are considered targets, legally.[141]

In an interview with Human Rights Watch, Hussein al-Sheikh, a Fatah official, made the same distinction. "We sent a message to al-Aqsa: 'Don't touch Israeli civilians. Never. Focus on the army and settlers. We don't consider settlers to be civilians.'"[142]

These assertions are inconsistent with international humanitarian law. The illegal status of settlements under international humanitarian law does not negate the rights of the civilians living there. The fact that a person lives in a settlement, whether legal or not, does not make him or her a legitimate military target. Under international humanitarian law, intentional attacks on civilians, or attacks that do not distinguish between military targets and civilians, are prohibited under all circumstances. Israeli civilians living in the settlements, so long as they do not take up arms and take an active part in hostilities, are noncombatants.

When individual settlers take an active part in hostilities, as opposed to acting in legitimate self-defense, they lose their civilian protection and become legitimate military targets during the period of their participation, just as Palestinian militants who take an active part in armed conflict become legitimate military targets during that period. However, even in a situation in which armed settlers were to become combatants, their presence among the larger civilian

---

[140] "No Israeli targets off-limits, Hamas spiritual chief warns," Flore de Preneuf interview with Shaikh Ahmad Yassin, *St. Petersburg Times* (Florida), August 11, 2001.

[141] Human Rights Watch interview, Gaza City, May 15, 2002.

[142] Human Rights Watch interview, Ramallah, May 14, 2002.

settler population would not negate the requirement that Palestinian combatants distinguish between military and civilian targets during that time, desist from attacking civilians, take all feasible precautions to avoid harm to civilians, and refrain from attacks that cause disproportionate harm to civilians.

All Israelis are Reservists

Hamas and Islamic Jihad further argue that Israel's military reservist system makes almost all of its Jewish citizens, except for children and the elderly, legitimate targets of armed attacks. "Are there civilians in Israel?" Shaikh Yassin asked in an *al-Hayat* interview, shortly after the end of Operation Defensive Shield.

> They are all in the military, men and women.... They wear civilian clothes inside Israel, and military clothes when they are with us.... The 20,000 or 30,000 reserve soldiers, where did they come from? Are they not part of the Israeli people? Were they not civilians?[143]

International humanitarian law makes clear, however, that reserve or off-duty soldiers who are not at that moment subject to the integrated disciplinary command of the armed forces are considered civilians until the time that they become subject to military command—meaning, until they are effectively incorporated into the armed forces. Their incorporation into the regular armed forces is most frequently signified by wearing a uniform or other identifiable insignia.

Imbalance of Means

Another justification offered by Palestinian armed groups for attacks against civilians is that the groups lack the weaponry and training available to the Israelis, and thus have no other means of fighting for the Palestinian cause. In an interview with the *Washington Post,* Hamas spokesman `Abd al-`Aziz al-Rantisi said:

> We don't have F-16s, Apache helicopters and missiles.... They are attacking us with weapons against which we can't defend ourselves. And now we have a weapon they can't defend themselves against....

---

[143] Fathi Sabbah, "Hamas leader to al-Hayat: Resistance, not reform, is the Palestinian demand right now," *al-Hayat,* May 22, 2002, translated in *Mideast Mirror* (London), May 22, 2002.

> We believe this weapon creates a kind of balance, because this
> weapon is like an F-16.[144]

Many Palestinians interviewed by Human Rights Watch said attacks on civilians were their only weapon with which to respond to repeated IDF use of tanks, attack helicopters, missiles, and warplanes.

Many conflicts, whether internal or international, take place between parties with radically differing means at their disposal. This is true of almost all wars that could potentially qualify under Additional Protocol I, article 4(1) as wars of national liberation, where one party frequently has vastly more sophisticated technical and military means than the other. Yet Protocol I reaffirms that all the basic rules of international humanitarian law still apply in those circumstances. Indeed, such a practice would be an exception that would virtually swallow the rules of international humanitarian law, since most wars are between forces of unequal means. The prohibition against intentional attacks against civilians is absolute. It cannot be justified by reference to a disparity of power between opposing forces.

Individual and Command Responsibility for Crimes Against Humanity and War Crimes

Under international law, persons who commit, order, or condone war crimes or crimes against humanity are criminally responsible individually for their actions. In certain circumstances, IHL also holds commanders criminally liable for war crimes or crimes against humanity committed by their subordinates.[145]

The responsibility of superior officers for atrocities by their subordinates is commonly known as command responsibility. Although the concept originated in military law, it now also includes the responsibility of civil authorities for abuses committed by persons under their direct authority.[146] The doctrine of command responsibility has been upheld in recent decisions by the international

---

[144] Molly Moore and John Ward Anderson, "Suicide Bombers Change Mideast's Military Balance," *Washington Post,* August 17, 2002.

[145] See Major-General (Retired) A.P.V. Rogers, "Command Responsibility Under the Law of War," lecture given at the Lauterpracht Resesarch Center for International Law, Cambridge University, 1999 at http://www.law.cam.ac.uk/RCIL/Archive.htm (accessed September 3, 2002).

[146] Article 28 of the Rome Statute of the International Criminal Court, "Responsibility of commanders and other superiors."

criminal tribunals for the former Yugoslavia and for Rwanda, and is codified in the Rome Statute for the International Criminal Court.

There are two forms of command responsibility. The first is direct responsibility for orders that are unlawful, such as when a military commander authorizes or orders rapes, massacres, or intentional attacks on civilians. The second is imputed responsibility, when a superior failed to prevent or punish crimes committed by a subordinate acting on his own initiative. This kind of responsibility depends on whether the superior had actual or constructive notice of the subordinates' crimes, and was in a position to stop and punish them.[147] If a commander had such notice, he can be held criminally responsible for his subordinates if he failed to take appropriate measures to control the subordinates, to prevent their atrocities, and to punish offenders.

For the doctrine of command responsibility to be applicable, two conditions must be met. A superior-subordinate relationship must exist, and the superior must exercise "effective control" over the subordinate. Effective control includes the ability to give orders or instructions, to ensure their implementation, and to punish or discipline subordinates if the orders are disobeyed. The International Criminal Tribunal for the former Yugoslavia (ICTY) in the "Celbici" case defined effective control as the superior "having the material ability to prevent and punish the commission" of violations of international humanitarian law.[148] The ICTY held that the

> [d]octrine of command responsibility is ultimately predicated upon the power of the superior to control the acts of his subordinates. A duty is placed upon the superior to exercise this power so as to prevent and repress the crimes committed by subordinates.... It follows that there is a threshold at which persons cease to possess the necessary powers of control over the actual perpetrators of offense and, accordingly, cannot properly be considered their "superiors".... [G]reat care must be taken lest an injustice be committed in holding individuals responsible for the acts of others in situations where the link of control is absent or too remote.[149]

---

[147] Constructive notice exists when offenses were so numerous or notorious that a reasonable person would conclude that the commander must have known of their commission.

[148] *Prosecutor v. Delali*, Judgment No. IT-96-21-T, Nov. 16,1998 (Celebici case), para. 378. See also *Prosecutor v. Karanac, Kunac and Vokovic.* Judgment No. IT-96-23-T & IT-96-23/1-T, Nov. 22, 2001, para. 396.

[149] Celebici, para. 377.

There is no statute of limitations for crimes against humanity or war crimes. Individuals who plan, organize, order, assist, commit or attempt to commit them can be prosecuted at any time, as can those with command responsibility for such acts. All states are obliged to bring to justice such persons, regardless of the place and time at which their crimes occurred. The Palestinian Authority, to the extent that it exercises authority, should take immediate steps to prevent the commission of such acts and to criminally prosecute the individuals who have ordered, organized, condoned, or carried them out.

The Participation of Children in Hostilities

International human rights and international humanitarian law have long prohibited the recruitment and use of children under fifteen years of age in hostilities.[150] There is growing international consensus that this threshold is too low, and that all children—internationally defined as those under the age of eighteen years—require increased protection from involvement in armed conflict.

As a result, in May 2000, the U.N. General Assembly adopted the Optional Protocol to the Convention on the Rights of the Child on the involvement of

---

[150] Article 77(2) of Protocol I requires parties to the conflict to "take all feasible measures in order that children who have not attained the age of fifteen years do not take a direct part in hostilities and, in particular, they shall refrain from recruiting them into their armed forces. In recruiting among those persons who have attained the age of fifteen years but who have not attained the age of eighteen years, the Parties to the conflict shall endeavor to give priority to those who are oldest." Article 38 of Convention on the Rights of the Child, adopted November 20, 1989, requires states parties to "take all feasible measures to ensure that persons who have not attained the age of fifteen years do not take a direct part in hostilities," and to "refrain from recruiting any person who has not attained the age of fifteen years into their armed forces." Similar provisions exist in international criminal law and international labor law. For example, article 8 of the Rome Statute of the ICC gives the court jurisdiction over the war crime of conscription or enlisting children under fifteen years into national armed forces or armed groups, or using them to participate actively in hostilities. Articles 1 and 3 of the International Labor Organization Convention no.182 includes the forced or compulsory recruitment of children under eighteen for use in armed conflict among the "worst forms of child labour" and requires states to "take immediate and effective measures to secure the prohibition and elimination of the worst forms of child labour as a matter of urgency." Convention concerning the Prohibition and Immediate Action for the Elimination of the Worst Forms of Child Labor, adopted June 17, 1999 (entered into force November 19, 2000).

children in armed conflict.[151] The Optional Protocol requires governments to take all feasible steps to ensure that children under the age of eighteen do not take direct part in hostilities; bans all compulsory recruitment of people under eighteen; and raises the minimum age for voluntary recruitment by governments. It also provides important additional protections against any recruitment or use of children under eighteen by armed groups that are not part of a state's armed forces. One hundred and ten states have signed the Optional Protocol since its adoption, and thirty-seven states have taken the necessary steps to ratify it.

The Optional Protocol states that "Armed groups that are distinct from the armed forces of a State should not, under any circumstances, recruit or use in hostilities persons under the age of 18 years." States Party are required to "take all feasible measures to prevent such recruitment and use, including the adoption of legal measures necessary to prohibit and criminalize such practices." These measures should also include "mak[ing] the principles and provisions of the present Protocol widely known and promoted by appropriate means, to adults and children alike," and taking "all feasible measures to ensure that persons within their jurisdiction recruited or used in hostilities contrary to the present Protocol are demobilized or otherwise released from service," including "when necessary, accord[ing] to such persons all appropriate assistance for their physical and psychological recovery and their social reintegration."[152]

Although the PA is not a party to the Convention on the Rights of the Child (CRC) or its Optional Protocol, it has signaled its willingness to accept its standards by endorsing the April 2001 Amman Declaration on the Use of Children as Soldiers, which stated that "the use in hostilities of any child under eighteen years of age by any armed force or armed group is unacceptable."[153]

---

[151] Optional Protocol to the Convention on the Rights of the Child on the involvement of children in armed conflict, adopted May, 2000. General Assembly resolution A/RES/54/263 (entered into force February 12, 2002).

[152] Ibid, articles 4(1), 4(2), 6(2), and 6(3).

[153] Amman Declaration on the Use of Children as Soldiers, April 10, 2001.

The PA also advocated the application of the Optional Protocol in a speech before the United Nations Special Session on Children in May 2002, emphasizing the urgency of the need to protect Palestinian children from the impact of armed conflict.[154] Human Rights Watch considers that, having made a moral commitment to the implementation of the CRC and its Optional Protocol, the PA should implement their provisions against the recruitment and use of children in hostilities.

---

[154] Statement of Dr. Emile Jarjou'i, Head of Delegation of the Observer Delegation of Palestine on the occasion of the Special Session of the General Assembly on Children, May 9, 2002 at www.un.org/ga/children/palestineE.htm (accessed June 6, 2002).

V. STRUCTURES AND STRATEGIES OF THE PERPETRATOR ORGANIZATIONS

Four Palestinian militant organizations have been responsible for almost all of the suicide bombing attacks against Israeli civilians during the current uprising: Hamas, Islamic Jihad, the al-Aqsa Martyrs' Brigades and the Popular Front for the Liberation of Palestine. Hamas and Islamic Jihad have pursued suicide bombings against civilians since the 1990s. The al-Aqsa Martyrs' Brigades and the PFLP began carrying out such attacks in 2002.

These same groups have been responsible for attacks against civilians using other means, such as targeted and indiscriminate shootings, which also constitute grave violations of international humanitarian law, as well as attacks against Israeli military targets. The following section discusses the structures and the public positions of these groups.

Human Rights Watch notes that leaders of each of these groups have demonstrated a significant degree of awareness of the fundamental norms of international humanitarian law. Three of the groups—Hamas, Islamic Jihad, and the PFLP—appear to be sufficiently well organized so as to be able to implement centralized policies that include upholding these fundamental norms. Therefore, in accordance with international law, and in particular the doctrine of command responsibility (discussed in section IV above), the leaders and those occupying positions of authority within these three groups can and should be held accountable for the war crimes and crimes against humanity that have been committed by members of their organizations. The same degree of organizational coherence and discipline does not appear to exist in the relationship between the al-Aqsa Martyrs' Brigades and Fatah. While the local leaders of the al-Aqsa Martyrs' Brigades are criminally responsible for crimes they ordered or oversaw, Fatah officials can be more appropriately said to bear a high degree of political responsibility for the crimes carried out in the name of their organization.

Two of the groups, Hamas and Islamic Jihad, have specifically sought to distinguish between their political or spiritual leaders and the commanders of their military wings—for example, Hamas's 'Izz al-Din al-Qassam Brigades or Islamic Jihad's Saraya al-Quds (Jerusalem Brigades). They have argued that specific decisions about the planning and carrying out of attacks are made by commanders of the military wings and that the overall political leadership is not privy to those decisions. However, criminal liability through command responsibility is not limited to the military chain of command. It also applies to political leaders, provided it can be shown that they exercise effective control over the subordinates who commit crimes under international law. As this

62

chapter demonstrates, the political leadership of these two groups have at times openly espoused, authorized, encouraged, or endorsed suicide attacks against civilians, and appear to have the authority to initiate or halt attacks as a matter of policy, even if they do not play a role in selecting specific targets.

For example, Ramadan `Abdullah Shalah, the Damascus-based secretary-general of Islamic Jihad, has repeatedly and publicly declared the movement's adherence to all forms of resistance, including suicide operations.[155] During the period since September 2000, Islamic Jihad has generally refused to commit itself publicly to cease-fires proclaimed by the PA, but the organization has nevertheless refrained from carrying out attacks against civilians inside Israel during several such periods, suggesting that the organization's leadership exercises a considerable measure of control over local groups. In the case of Hamas, there is abundant evidence that the military wing is accountable to a political steering committee that includes Shaikh Ahmad Yassin, the group's acknowledged "spiritual" leader, as well as spokespersons such as Ismail Abu Shanab, `Abd al-`Aziz al-Rantisi, and Mahmud Zahar. Yassin himself, as well as Salah Shehadah, the late founder and commander of the `Izz al-Din al-Qassam Brigades, have confirmed in public remarks that the military wing implements policies that are set by the political wing.

The PFLP also has a centralized political command structure. The organization has at no point argued that its military wing, the Martyr Abu `Ali Mustafa Brigade, is acting independently from the political leadership.

The al-Aqsa Martyrs' Brigades, by contrast, emerged in late 2000 and early 2001 in refugee camps among militants who claimed an affiliation with Fatah, the largest Palestinian political organization. The available public evidence and testimony suggests that al-Aqsa Martyrs' Brigades militants take decisions under loose, personality-driven local command structures, with a degree of autonomy and improvisation not characteristic of the other organizations.

To the extent that the leaders of Hamas and Islamic Jihad may not have directly ordered or authorized specific suicide bombing attacks on civilians, the sustained and frequent nature of these attacks and the public claims of responsibility by the groups that have carried them out remove any doubt that the leaders of both groups are aware that their subordinates were carrying out these attacks. Although suicide bombings by the PFLP have been much less frequent, there are no grounds for thinking that the leadership is not aware when members carry out such attacks against civilians. In all three cases, these leaders thus had a duty to use all available means to try to stop their subordinates from

---

[155] See for example, Ibrahim Hamidi, "Shalah to al-Hayat: We have not sensed a change in the Syrian position towards the resistance," *al-Hayat*, May 14, 2002 (in Arabic).

committing these crimes—a duty that, as described below, they have failed to fulfill. The leadership of Fatah similarly failed to use their political influence to end such attacks by the al-Aqsa Martyrs' Brigades.

Hamas (*harakat al-muqawama al-islamiyya*, Islamic Resistance Movement)

Since September 2000, Hamas has carried out more suicide bombing attacks on civilians than any other Palestinian group. Hamas was founded at the outset of the "first intifada" against Israeli military occupation, in December 1987. It emerged as a militant and activist offshoot of the Palestinian branch of the Muslim Brotherhood, which had traditionally avoided the activism and political violence pursued by Fatah and other secular Palestinian nationalist groups.[156]

The Hamas bombings have been the most destructive in human terms, killing at least 168 persons, 153 of whom were civilians, and injuring more than 949. Hamas suicide bombings include some of the most notorious attacks, such as the Tel Aviv nightclub attack of June 1, 2001, which killed twenty-one, mostly teenagers; the Sbarro pizzeria bombing in Jerusalem on August 9, 2001, which killed fifteen; the March 27, 2002 bombing of the Seder in Netanya which killed twenty-eight; and the June 18, 2002 bombing of a crowded commuter bus in southern Jerusalem which killed nineteen.

Background

Hamas is frequently described as a nationalist, Islamist social movement. It has strong roots in the Palestinian lower middle class as well as in the Palestinian intelligentsia. The movement has a three-part identity: political, military, and social. Hamas, as a distinctive political movement, explicitly opposes many PA and Fatah policies. One knowledgeable Israeli analyst described Hamas as "an authentic product of Palestinian society under Israeli rule, more so than the PA." [157] Hamas's image and popularity are significantly

---

[156] On the origins of Hamas as a political and social movement, see Ziad Abu-Amr, *Islamic Fundamentalism in the West Bank and Gaza* (Bloomington: Indiana University Press, 1994); Shaul Mishal and Avraham Sela, *The Palestinian Hamas: Vision, Violence, and Coexistence* (New York: Columbia University Press, 2000); and Graham Usher, "What Kind of Nation? The Rise of Hamas in the Occupied Territories," in Joel Beinin and Joe Stork (ed.s), *Political Islam: Essays from Middle East Report* (Berkeley and Los Angeles: University of California Press, 1997).

[157] Human Rights Watch interview with Reuven Paz, former academic director of the International Policy Institute for Counter-Terrorism Research, Herzliya, June 9, 2002. In the mid-1990s, Paz was head of research for Israel's General Intelligence Service (Shin Bet). He is presently the director of the Project for the Study of Radical Islam.

enhanced by its wide network of community-level charitable and welfare societies, some of which provide essential services that the PA does not provide. Its military wing, the `Izz al-Din al-Qassam Brigades, has been in operation since 1991.[158] One Israeli press account, apparently based on intelligence reports, estimated that Hamas's military wing had 150 members in Gaza and roughly sixty to ninety members in the West Bank in mid-2001.[159] Hamas supporters are commonly thought to number in the tens of thousands.

In its charter, Hamas defines itself as a chapter of the Muslim Brotherhood in Palestine: a "unique Palestinian movement" that "owes its loyalty to God, derives from Islam its way of life, and strives to raise the banner of God over every inch of Palestine."[160] As stated in article 12:

> Nothing is loftier or deeper in nationalism than a struggle [jihad] against the enemy and confronting him when he sets foot on the land of the Muslims.... Whereas other nationalisms consist of material, human, or territorial considerations, the Islamic Resistance Movement's nationalism carries all of that plus all the more important divine factors.

Hamas's charter effectively appropriates Palestinian territorial nationalism— once considered a form of idolatry by traditional Islamist movements such as the Muslim Brotherhood—as a function of religious belief.[161] Also political, rather than religious, is the apparent Hamas goal of supplanting Fatah as the leading political and social force in the Palestinian territories.

---

[158] Shaikh `Izz al-Din al-Qassam, of Syrian origin, lived and worked among displaced and landless Palestinian peasants in the Haifa area in the 1920s and 1930s, and was killed in a clash with British troops in November 1935. His death and funeral helped spark the 1936-39 Palestinian Arab revolt. See Rashid Khalidi, *Palestinian Identity: The Construction of Modern National Consciousness* (New York: Columbia University Press, 1997), p. 115. Khalidi characterizes the shaikh as "the first articulate public apostle of armed rural resistance" to Jewish settlements in Palestine.

[159] Yo'av Limor, "Terror Map of HAMAS and Islamic Jihad," *Ma'ariv* (Shabat Supplement), August 17, 2001, translated in FBIS, Near East and South Asia, August 20, 2001, FBIS-NES-2001-0817.

[160] All citations of the charter are based on the translation reproduced as Appendix Two in Mishal and Sela, *The Palestinian Hamas.*

[161] Graham Usher characterizes the charter as "blend[ing] a socially puritanical version of Islam, an accommodation to PLO nationalism, and a rehash of Eurocentric anti-Semitism." "What Kind of Nation?" p. 340.

Involvement in Suicide Bombings

On April 6, 1994, a Hamas member carried out the first suicide bombing against Israeli civilians. The attack, in the northern city of Afula, killed eight and wounded thirty-four. The attack took place at the end of the mourning period for twenty-nine Palestinians killed at prayer in Hebron's Ibrahim mosque by an Israeli settler, Baruch Goldstein. It also appeared to have been timed to disrupt negotiations between Israel and the PLO over the implementation of the Oslo Declaration of Principles. Between 1994 and 1998, Hamas carried out further attacks to disrupt Israeli-Palestinian negotiations, enhance its position *vis-a-vis* other Palestinian factions, and undermine the Palestinian Authority.

When suicide bombing attacks against civilians resumed, in the early months of 2001, Hamas was in the forefront. Between January 2001 and July 31, 2002, the organization's military wing, the `Izz al-Din al-Qassam Brigades, claimed responsibility for eighteen suicide bomb attacks against Israeli civilians, more than any other armed group. "They didn't find many recruits back in the nineties, when Hamas pioneered these attacks," a Palestinian journalist in the West Bank told Human Rights Watch. "The intifada, the Israeli siege, changed all that."[162]

PA leaders have complained, and Hamas leaders have acknowledged, that Hamas's suicide bombings and other attacks against civilians may be couched in the language of retaliation, but are also intended to influence actual or potential Israeli-Palestinian political negotiations. One example was the March 27, 2002 attack on the Park Hotel in Netanya, which killed twenty-nine and wounded more than one hundred. "Our operation coincided with the Arab summit in Beirut," the Hamas communiqué noted, and "is a clear message to our Arab rulers that our struggling people have chosen their road and know how to regain lands and rights in full, depending only on God."[163]

The Islamic Jihad's spokesperson, Mahmud Zahar, in an interview with the *New York Times*, also cited the late March 2002 negotiations conducted by General Anthony Zinni, special advisor to U.S. Secretary of State Colin Powell, to secure a cease-fire. "The Zinni mission was bad for us," he said, noting that its proposed terms included the disarmament of groups such as Hamas and the arrest of their leaders.[164] Hamas's rivalry with the Palestinian Authority also

---

[162] Human Rights Watch interview, name withheld, Nablus, June 7, 2002.

[163] Translated from Arabic by Human Rights Watch.

[164] Joel Brinkley, "Arabs' grief in Bethlehem, bombers' gloating in Gaza," *New York Times*, April 4, 2002.

plays a role. "Our goal is not just to target Israelis but also Abu `Ammar," Ismail Abu Shanab told Human Rights Watch, referring to President Yasir Arafat.[165]

In late May 2002, Hassan Yusuf, a West Bank Hamas spokesperson, highlighted another tactical perspective when he told the *Washington Post*, "The [suicide attacks] are not a goal, they are a means. They are not sacred. They can be reviewed. But in exchange for what? For an end to the Israeli aggression against us.... You've got to discuss the basis of the problem. And the basis of the problem is the occupation."[166]

During the same period, Hamas's "spiritual leader" Shaikh Yassin was asked if the group's leadership had discussed the option of stopping these attacks. "There is no subject that is not discussed within the movement," he told *al-Hayat*. "Every development is discussed. At the end, we reach common decisions."[167]

These and other comments demonstrate that the Hamas leadership has pursued attacks against civilians as a conscious policy. A group that pursues multiple, intentional attacks against civilians as a matter of policy is responsible for crimes against humanity. Hamas political and military leaders alike can be held individually criminally responsible for these acts because of their direct complicity. In addition, in light of their ability to control the use of suicide bombing attacks against civilians in broad terms, they can be held criminally responsible under the doctrine of command responsibility.

Structure

The Hamas leadership is located both inside and outside the Occupied Territories. The "internal" leadership consists of a Gaza-based steering committee that includes, in addition to Shaikh Yassin, Ismail Abu Shanab, Mahmud Zahar, and `Abd al-`Aziz al-Rantisi. This leadership is reportedly linked to the West Bank via a coordinating committee.[168] The "external" leadership, in the form of the organization's Political Bureau, was especially instrumental in determining social, political, and military policies until the late

---

[165] Human Rights Watch interview with Ismail Abu Shanab, Gaza City, May 15, 2002.

[166] Edward Cody, "Unclear U.S. Role Leaves Middle East Process at Impass," *Washington* Post, May 22, 2002.

[167] Fathi Sabbah, "Hamas leader to al-Hayat: Resistance, not reform, is the Palestinian demand right now," *al-Hayat*, May 22, 2002, translated in *Mideast Mirror* (London), May 22, 2002.

[168] Mishal and Sela, *The Palestinian Hamas,* p. 58. The book also includes as Appendix One a chart indicating Hamas's internal structure, in which most of the links between institutions and sectors are informal.

1990s. The balance between internal and external leadership reportedly shifted following Israel's release from detention of Shaikh Yassin in 1997 and the Jordanian government's subsequent crackdown on Hamas activities there in August 1999.[169] The enhanced influence of the "internal" Gaza-based leadership of Hamas, along with more effective security cooperation between Palestinian and Israeli security services, contributed to a halt in suicide attacks against Israeli civilians in the 1999-2000 period.[170]

The "external" leadership, the Political Bureau, includes bureau chief Khalid Mish'al and deputy chief Musa Abu Marzuq and now operates from Damascus. The continued influence of the external Political Bureau is reflected in reports that it, along with the group's military cadres, "looked askance" at recent negotiations in Gaza among all Palestinian factions, including Hamas, to come up with a joint platform that would, among other things, subject all the groups to unified leadership and policies and confine "resistance activities" to the West Bank and Gaza Strip.[171]

Hamas activities in the West Bank have traditionally been centered in the Nablus area in the north, including an-Najah University, and the Hebron area in the south. Several sources interviewed by Human Rights Watch said there is no single Hamas leadership on the West Bank. Instead, each area has separate links to Gaza and Damascus, and also receives public legitimization from externally based religious authorities such as Shaikh Yusuf Qardawi, an influential Egyptian-born cleric living in Qatar.[172] The organization also has links with Iran

---

[169] For an account of Yassin's release and the circumstances that preceded it, see "Israel releases nine prisoners in deal for Mossad agents," CNN, October 13, 1997 at http://www.cnn.com/WORLD/9710/13/israel.hamas/ (accessed September 3, 2002).

[170] Israeli analyst Reuven Paz, writing in December 1999, judged that the Amman-based Hamas leadership "has placed greater emphasis on the military side of the struggle—concentrating mainly in the struggle against Israel rather than on gaining the local support of the Palestinian society in the Territories." See Reuven Paz, "Hamas Analyzes its Terrorist Activity," International Policy Institute for Counter-Terrorism (ICT), December 21, 1999 at http://www.ict.org.il (accessed September 3, 2002). Ely Karmon, another analyst with the ICT, wrote that the reason for the decline in attacks by Hamas and Islamic Jihad in that period "was due to the combined preventive counter-terrorist policy of the PA and Israel." Ely Karmon, "Hamas' Terrorism Strategy: Operational Limitations and Political Constraints," *Middle East Review of International Affairs,* vol. 4, no. 1 (March 2000), p.66.

[171] Graham Usher, "Cease-fires that cannot be," *Middle East International,* August 16, 2002.

[172] Shaikh al-Qardawi appears frequently on the Qatar-based al-Jazeera television network. According to a Jazeera transcript of a broadcast on December 11, 2001, Shaikh al-Qardawi said, "Palestinians are resisting occupation and therefore have the right to use all means to defend their rights." He disputed "those who say that these operations target

and the Hizbollah movement in Lebanon, dating back to Israel's December 1992 expulsion to south Lebanon of some 415 Palestinian Islamist activists, most of them affiliated with Hamas.[173]

Despite its geographical spread, the Hamas leadership appears to be well organized and effective, capable of pursuing consistent policies and enforcing compliance with instructions. Shaikh Yassin and other Hamas leaders have confirmed that decision-making responsibility in Hamas lies with the political leadership. In a June 6, 2001 interview, for example, Yassin disputed reports that the `Izz al-Din al-Qassam Brigades had declared a truce. "The political wing, not the military wing, drafts the policies of Hamas," Yassin said. "The military wing implements the policies that are drawn up by the political wing." In the same interview, Yassin attempted to disclaim any personal responsibility for the suicide bombing attacks on the grounds that he was not involved in "planning" them. "[Israel] knows more than anyone else that Shaikh Ahmad Yassin has nothing to do with the planning of suicide operations," he said. "Military work needs experts. I spend all the day in meetings and audiences with people. How can I plan suicide operations when my house is always full of citizens and people who come seeking solutions to their problems?"[174] However, Yassin did not deny authorizing attacks.

The late founder and head of the `Izz al-Din al-Qassam Brigades, Salah Shehadah, also confirmed the primacy of the Hamas steering committee over the

---

civilians," arguing that "they have militarized the society so that all Israeli men and women are soldiers...." See transcript, "The Intifada and Suicide bombing" at http://www.al-jazeera.com/programs/shareea/articles/2001/12/12-11-1 (accessed April 23, 2002). In an April 4, 2001 broadcast, Shaikh al-Qardawi took issue with the judgment of a high Saudi Arabian religious official criticizing suicide attacks against civilians as not legitimate, arguing the need to distinguish "between suicide as an egotistic practice and suicide bombing as a last resort weapon and a defense of one's community and religion." See "Al-Qardawi: martyrdom operations are among the greatest forms of Jihad" at http://www.al-jazeera.com/news/arabic/2001/4/4-22-9 (accessed April 23, 2002).

[173] Then-Prime Minister Yitzhak Rabin ordered the summary expulsions after Hamas claimed responsibility for killing five Israeli soldiers and policemen in a one-week period, including the murder in custody of a captured border policeman. The deportees remained camped near the Israeli border for most of 1993. Some 181 of the detainees were allowed to return in August 1993, and others subsequently. Israeli analyst Reuven Paz sees Hamas as drawing increasing political support from Iran, despite the movement's overwhelmingly Sunni character. Human Rights Watch interview with Reuven Paz, Herzliya, June 9, 2002.

[174] "Hamas Founder Yasin on Cease-fire, Suicide Operations, Ties with Hizballah," *al-Mujalla* (London), June 17-23, 2001. Translated from Arabic in Foreign Broadcast Information Service (FBIS), Near East and South Asia, June 17, 2001.

military wing in terms of authorizing attacks on civilians. In an on-line chat posted on the 'Izz al-Din al-Qassam website prior to his assassination on July 23, 2002, Shehadah said:

> We are the soldiers of the military wing, and the political wing does not tell us to do that or this, or execute this operation or that. However, the vision of the political wing is what we follow at the military section, and the political decisions have authority over the military wing....[175]

In the same discussion, Shehadah said the respective regional military wings recommended "martyrs" to the main leadership, which made a final decision.[176]

Salim Hija, described by the Israeli authorities as "a senior West Bank Hamas activist," was captured by the IDF in April 2002. The IDF has published extracts of what it says is Hija's interrogation, in which the Hamas structure is described as "small compartmentalized squads" that receive instructions from Hamas leaders in the West Bank and abroad.[177] A well-informed Palestinian journalist told Human Rights Watch that the current clashes had at least initially enhanced the role of some local Hamas leaders. Jamal Mansur, the Hamas leader in Nablus until he was assassinated in July 2001, was "more important than [Damascus-based Khalid] Mish'al," he said, while noting that "local decisions are referred to a higher level" before being implemented.[178] Qadura Musa, a

---

[175] "The Leader of the Military Wing of Hamas Reveals for the First Time The Secrets of the Martyrs, Their Operations and Their Weapons" (in Arabic) at http://www.qassam.net/chat/salah3.html (accessed June 15 2002). Translated by Human Rights Watch.

[176] Ibid. Shehadah said the organization bases its decision on various criteria, including piety, "detachment from the material world," honesty, obedience, courage, and dedication. "We may sometimes make mistakes in selecting people," he said. On Shehadah's role in Hamas, see http://www.palestine-info.co.uk/hamas/index.htm (accessed October 10, 2002). For the Human Rights Watch statement on the fourteen civilian casualties that occurred as a result of the IDF killing of Shehadah, see Human Rights Watch press release, "Israeli Airstrike on Crowded Civilian Area Condemned," July 23, 2002 at http://www.hrw.org/press/2002/07/gaza072302.htm.

[177] Appendix F, *Confession from the Interrogation of Salim Hija, Senior West Bank Hamas Activist*, in IDF compilation, "Nablus the Infrastructure Center of Palestinian Terrorism" at http://www.idf.il/arafat/schem/english/main_index.stm (accessed October 8, 2002).

[178] Human Rights Watch interview, name withheld, Nablus, June 7, 2002.

Fatah leader in Jenin, told Human Rights Watch, "When we needed political decisions from Hamas, we asked Jamal Mansur and Jamal Salim."[179]

Hamas publishes a monthly magazine, *Filastin al-Muslimah*, in London, and maintains websites in both Arabic and English.[180]

Islamic Jihad

Like Hamas, but some years earlier, Islamic Jihad rose out of the Muslim Brotherhood organization.[181] Islamic Jihad was founded in 1982 by students at the Islamic University in Gaza, although the name was formally adopted only in 1987.[182]

Unlike Hamas, whose ideology calls for the "liberation" of all of historic Palestine, Islamic Jihad sees the struggle for Palestine as a catalyst for an Islamic revolution throughout the Arab world.[183] Its most influential founders were Fathi `Abd al-`Aziz al-Shikaki, a physician from the Rafah area of the Gaza Strip, and Shaikh `Abd al-`Aziz `Awda, from Gaza's Jabalya refugee camp.

---

[179] Human Rights Watch interview, Jenin refugee camp, June 10, 2002. Mansur and Salim were killed when an IDF helicopter gunship fired a missile into their office in a Nablus apartment building on July 31, 2001. The attack killed three other Hamas members, a journalist, two children, and injured several dozen.

[180] Accessible sites include http://www.fm-m.com (website of *Filastin al-Muslimah*, the Hamas-affiliated monthly magazine mentioned above), http://www.palestine-info.co.uk/index_e.htm and http://www.palestine-info.info/arabic/hamas/index.htm (accessed October 10, 2002). Other sites have been blocked, including http://www.qassem.net and http://www.palestine-info.com.

[181] On the origins of the Palestinian Islamic Jihad, see Meir Hatina, *Islam and Salvation in Palestine* (Tel Aviv: Tel Aviv University, 2001) and Ziad Abu `Amr, *Islamic Fundamentalism in the West Bank and Gaza* (Bloomington and Indianapolis: Indiana University Press, 1994).

[182] Reuven Paz, "Higher Education and the Development of Palestinian Islamic Groups," *Middle East Review of International Affairs* vol. 4, no.2 (June 2000).

[183] "The Palestine problem is the central issue of the modern Islamic movements" was a leading Islamic Jihad slogan. Hatina, *Islam and Salvation*, p. 32. Abu `Amr cites a 1980 publication reflecting Islamic Jihad's analysis that the present condition of Palestinians owed to "the opportunistic non-Islamic leaderships, which successively led the masses, or which seized power following the defeat of the Islamic state at the beginning of this century," and that the Arab nationalist movement "was a legitimate son of the Western assault against the Islamic nation," as was the Zionist movement. Abu `Amr, *Islamic Fundamentalism*, p. 105.

Background

Islamic Jihad was influenced by, and interacted with, radical Egyptian Islamists in the 1980s, many of whom were inspired by Iran's Islamic revolution. The organization comprised for the most part young men, most with higher academic or professional degrees, who saw themselves as forming an elite vanguard rather than a broad community-based movement along the lines of Hamas, although the organization also maintained a civic component in the Gaza Strip. Islamic Jihad also recruited former activists from Fatah and the Palestine Liberation Army of the PLO; and Islamic Jihad students from Gaza attracted adherents in West Bank university towns such as Nablus, Ramallah, and Hebron.[184] In addition, prisons proved to be important recruiting grounds. Early on, the organization established small clandestine cells to carry out armed attacks against Israeli targets, both military and civilian. Islamic Jihad's tactical links with Fatah in the West Bank came under severe strain after the November 1988 "two-state" decision of the Palestine National Council, which Islamic Jihad dismissed as a "contaminated peace" that would "divide the homeland, the homeland of faith."[185]

Islamic Jihad's own "introduction" states as its main principle: "Palestine—from the river to the sea—an Arab, Islamic land whose jurisdiction prohibits giving up any inch of its land." The same document defines the goal as "preparing the Palestinian people for martyrdom as well as preparing them politically and militarily and in all educational, cultural and organizational methods ...to qualify them to carry on their martyrdom duties toward Palestine."[186] Ramadan Shalah, the organization's secretary-general, in a published contribution to an "internal debate," defined "the goal of the Islamic movement within Palestine" as "Liberating Palestine, all of Palestine, and eliminating the Zionist state within it."[187] In a May 2002 interview in Beirut, Shalah reaffirmed that "[w]here we are concerned, the whole of Palestine is occupied territory," but added: "In the current intifada, however, all Palestinian

---

[184] Hatina, *Islam and Salvation*, pp. 23-28.

[185] Ibid., Islamic Jihad manifesto, p. 68.

[186] See "Introduction to the movement and its vision" (in Arabic) at http://www.qudsway.com (accessed October 10, 2002). Translated by Human Rights Watch

[187] The Oslo agreement, Shehadah also wrote, "demolished the foundations of the Palestinian resistance.... The Islamic movement entered a period of crisis that had more or less led to the breakdown of its military infrastructure, where it lost most of its human and financial resources." See *al-Intiqad* (Lebanese weekly), no. 924, March 2002 (in Arabic) at http://www.qudsway.com. Translated by Human Rights Watch.

factions including Islamic Jihad are agreed that the objective of Palestinian resistance today is to roll back Israel's occupation of the West Bank and Gaza unconditionally."[188]

Islamic Jihad's strong affiliation with the revolutionary character of the Islamic Republic of Iran was enhanced by the Rabin government's expulsion of some 415 Palestinian Islamist militants, mostly Hamas supporters but including about fifty Islamic Jihad militants as well, to south Lebanon in December 1992. There, "its proximity to Hizbollah turned the movement into a quasi-military organization," and Islamic Jihad carried out attacks on Israeli forces in south Lebanon, including some joint attacks with Hizbollah.[189] These years appear to have solidified a pattern of Iranian patronage of the organization that reportedly continues to the present.[190]

Involvement in Suicide Bombings

In the aftermath of the Oslo Accords, Islamic Jihad revived its campaign of attacks against Israeli targets, which included suicide bombings against civilians as well as military targets. In a presentation on its website about its military wing, Saraya al-Quds, Islamic Jihad asserts that the formation of a military wing dates from 1992, "when the martyr Mahmud al-Khawaja established an organized military agency to replace the different unorganized, individual groups."[191] This statement also claims that "the military wing of Jihad was the first to introduce those tactics," referring to suicide bombers (*istishadiyiin*).[192] A

---

[188] Ibrahim Hamidi, "Islamic Jihad reiterates possibility of end to attacks on civilians," *Daily Star* (Beirut), May 16, 2002.

[189] Hatina, *Islam and Salvation*, pp. 110-11.

[190] Hatina cites al-Shikaki's denial that most of the organization's resources were provided by Iran, and notes that this patronage "did not necessarily mean the receipt of total or unequivocal loyalty." Ibid., pp. 111-12. Independent Palestinian analysts, as well as leaders of other Palestinian organizations and the Palestinian Authority, told Human Rights Watch that in the northern West Bank, Islamic Jihad did not lack for financial resources. Haidar Irshaid, the deputy governor of Jenin, said he "was not authorized" to give the PA view of this matter but did say he had "heard" that Islamic Jihad funding in the area came from Iran and Syria. Human Rights Watch interview with Haidar Irshaid, Jenin, June 10, 2002.

[191] "From Qassam to Saraya al-Quds," *al-Intiqad*, no. 924 (in Arabic) at http://www.qudsway.com (accessed October 3, 2002). Translated by Human Rights Watch.

[192] Ibid. In this account Islamic Jihad writes that, "the main obstacle faced by Qassam was that their members were being detained by the Palestinian Authority." The account contends that PA torture of one Jihad member led to the identification and subsequent assassination (on July 22, 1995 in Gaza) of Mahmud al-Khawaja, "one of the most vital

January 1995 attack killed twenty IDF soldiers at the Beit Lid junction near Netanya. Al-Shikaki, in a March 1995 interview, stressed the need for "unconventional" means to create a "balance of fear" that would help to offset Israel's conventional military power.[193] The Israeli assassination of al-Shikaki in Malta in October 1995 was followed by two suicide attacks against IDF forces in Gaza. Islamic Jihad then began attacking civilians. An attack in Tel Aviv in March 1996 killed twelve civilians and wounded about one hundred. Ramadan Shalah, another Islamic Jihad founding member of Gazan origins, succeeded al-Shikaki and remains today the secretary-general of the group, based in Damascus.[194]

Islamic Jihad's Saraya al-Quds claimed responsibility for the first suicide bombing attack, against a military target, following the outbreak of the current clashes. On October 26, 2000, Nabil Farraj al-Arrir, an Islamic law student, rammed his bicycle against an IDF outpost near the Gush Katif settlement bloc, blowing himself up and lightly wounding a soldier. The date marked the fifth anniversary of the assassination of Islamic Jihad founder Fathi `Abd al-`Aziz al-Shikaki. In a statement broadcast by al-Manar, the Lebanon-based television of Hizbollah, Islamic Jihad Secretary General Ramadan Shalah said, "[T]argeting the Israeli army in its fortified post by the *mujahid* this morning confirms that our option is jihad and we always target the Zionist army. If we wanted to kill civilians as this enemy is doing, it would have been easier for us."[195]

Islamic Jihad's subsequent attacks revealed Shalah's commitment not to attack civilians as hollow. Between May 2001 and July 2002, Islamic Jihad carried out at least ten suicide attacks targeting civilians, or in circumstances where it was impossible to distinguish between civilians and legitimate military targets. At least twenty-eight civilians were killed in these attacks, and some 326 were wounded. According to Ramadan Shalah, Islamic Jihad's current rationale for attacks inside Israel is that "the Palestinian territories occupied in 1948 constitute the power base for the Israeli entity. It is from there that the tanks and

---

members of Jihad." According to Israeli analyst Meir Hatina, "Not surprisingly, members of the Islamic Jihad were the first to be imprisoned by the PA security forces in early 1994 and charged with 'harming the security of the homeland and the agreements signed by the PA.'" Hatina, *Islam and Salvation*, p. 88.

[193] The interview in *al-Sharq al-Awsat* of March 17, 1995, is cited in ibid., pp. 87-88.

[194] In the early 1990s, Shalah taught at South Florida University and headed the Tampa-based Institute for Research of Islam and the Middle East. He relocated to Beirut in 1994 and then to Damascus upon succeeding al-Shikaki as head of Islamic Jihad.

[195] "Islamic Jihad secretary threatens more attacks against Israeli troops," al-Manar television (Lebanon), BBC Monitoring Middle East, October 26, 2000.

planes come to bomb our villages and towns and kill our people."[196] As noted above, this rationalization violates basic principles of international humanitarian law.

Structure

Islamic Jihad shares many features with Hamas, including its opposition to the Oslo Accords and its secretive, disciplined structure. According to one well-informed Palestinian journalist in the northern West Bank, "In Hamas and [Islamic] Jihad, nothing is done without a high-level decision from the top, and from outside [the West Bank], even if the initiative is local."[197] "The Islamic Jihad secretary-general and other key figures are based in Damascus. While Islamic Jihad is sharply critical of PA policies, it does not, unlike Hamas, seek to rival Arafat and Fatah as the dominant Palestinian political force. Islamic Jihad is at least nominally a member of the Palestine Liberation Organization and is represented on the 124-member PLO Central Council.[198]

The clandestine, cell-based structure of the organization has made it difficult to estimate the size of Islamic Jihad. Palestinian analyst Ziad Abu `Amr, writing about the years of the first intifada, said that the organization's supporters, "despite their small numbers compared to Hamas, were found all across the West Bank and Gaza."[199] Israeli analyst Reuven Paz estimated that Islamic Jihad's total numbers in the Occupied Territories during the current clashes probably were in the range of three to four hundred.[200] The organization's presence today appears strongest in Gaza and in the Jenin district in the northern West Bank.[201]

---

[196] Ibrahim Hamidi, "Islamic Jihad reiterates possibility of end to attacks on civilians," *Daily Star* (Beirut), May 16, 2002.

[197] Human Rights Watch interview, name withheld, Nablus, June 7, 2002.

[198] The two representatives are Ma'mun Asac al-Tamimi and Ibrahim Kamil al-Itr. For an updated list of the Central Council as elected by the twenty-first session of the Palestine National Council in April 1996, see http://www.middleeast.reference.users.btopenworld.com.plocc (accessed August 7, 2002).

[199] Abu `Amr, *Islamic Fundamentalism,* p. 96.

[200] Human Rights Watch interview with Reuven Paz, Herzliya, June 9, 2002.

[201] "From Qassam to Saraya al-Quds" at http:// www.qudsway.com, refers to Jenin as "a dynamic center and storage house for [Islamic] Jihad, as the enemy frequently points out." This account also asserts that all but one of the Islamic Jihad suicide bombers had come from the Jenin refugee camp (accessed October 3, 2002).

Islamic Jihad's attacks against civilians included joint attacks with Hamas (the Sbarro bombing attack, on August 9, 2001) and with the al-Aqsa Martyrs' Brigades (a shooting attack on November 27, 2001). According to Palestinian intelligence documents made public by the IDF, Islamic Jihad and al-Aqsa Brigades members in Jenin enjoyed an unusually close relationship, in which Islamic Jihad sometimes undertook joint operations with al-Aqsa Martyrs' Brigades members and allegedly gave them financial support.

A leader of the attacks launched by Islamic Jihad from Jenin was Mahmud Tawalba, aged twenty-four, who was killed on April 8 during the IDF assault on the Jenin refugee camp. His mother told Human Rights Watch that those "who carried out bombings would go to Mahmud. He was in charge for more than one year after the intifada started." According to his mother, Tawalba had left school after the ninth grade and worked as a pipe fitter and plasterer. In the late 1990s, he worked for several years in Israel.[202] Five years ago, she said, he became increasingly religious and opened a shop selling religious cassettes in Jenin city. "Even before the intifada, he was thinking about paradise, thinking about a martyr operation," she said.

Tawalba searched out the Islamic Jihad organization, his mother said, rather than having been recruited. He received money from the organization, but she said she believed it was not a significant amount. "He got some money from Islamic Jihad but continued to work. He turned over the organization's money to the poor. He never had more than one hundred shekels in his pocket. He was satisfied, only thinking about martyrdom."[203] She said that at first she had urged him to express his religiosity in other ways—"to build a mosque"—but that she came to support fully the "martyr operations." Another son, Murad, is currently serving a thirteen-year term in an Israeli prison after he was caught by Israeli security services on his way to carry out a "martyr operation," having been dispatched, she said, by Mahmud.

Ramadan Shalah, Islamic Jihad's secretary-general, has indicated on a number of occasions that attacks against civilians represent the policy of the organization as determined by its leadership. "We have already made many offers to reconsider our policy of targeting Israeli civilians inside Israel proper in exchange for Israel reversing its policy of killing Palestinian civilians," he told

---

[202] Jenin is directly adjacent to Israel's border with the West Bank, close to the Israeli town of Afula and not far from Haifa and the Galilee region. According to residents, a very large proportion of its workforce commuted to jobs in Israel prior to the outbreak of clashes in September 2000.

[203] Human Rights Watch interview with Mahmud Tawalba's mother, Jenin, June 11, 2002.

an interviewer in May 2002.[204] Shalah reaffirmed the group's intent to continue suicide bombings in a speech in Tehran few weeks later. According to *al-Hayat*'s summary of Shalah's remarks, the Islamic Jihad leader said that "the source of the ["martyrdom"] operations was Damascus," where Shalah is based, though "the planning and strategizing were all internally done."[205]

The al-Aqsa Martyrs' Brigades

The al-Aqsa Martyrs' Brigades emerged following the outbreak of Israeli-Palestinian clashes in September 2000 and consists of local clusters of armed activists, most of whom are apparently affiliated with Fatah. The impetus for the formation of the al-Aqsa Brigades came from militants residing in the Balata refugee camp, near Nablus, in late 2000 or early 2001.[206] The al-Aqsa Martyrs' Brigades have claimed responsibility for attacks against Israeli military targets and also for several major indiscriminate shooting attacks against Israeli civilians inside Israel, including one in Afula in November 2001 and a second at a bat mitzvah in Hadera in January 2002, as well as multiple shooting attacks against Israeli settlers.[207]

The al-Aqsa Brigades claimed responsibility for at least twelve of the thirty-eight suicide bombing attacks against Israeli civilians in the January-August 2002 period. Unlike Hamas and Islamic Jihad, the al-Aqsa Martyrs' Brigades are linked to the ruling faction in the Palestinian Authority, rather than the political rivals of the PA and Fatah. The al-Aqsa Brigades' attacks against civilians have been considered by many—including the Israeli authorities—to reflect an official policy of support for suicide attacks against civilians by the leadership of Fatah, and, by extension, the PA.

---

[204] Hamidi, "Islamic Jihad reiterates possibility of end to attacks on civilians," *Daily Star*.

[205] Ibrahim Hamidi, "Shalah to al-Hayat: Our declaration from Damascus is a confirmation of the internal performance of our military wing," *al-Hayat*, June 6, 2002.

[206] See for example, Matthew McAllester, "A potent, deadly militia," *Newsday*, March 10, 2002; Suzanne Goldenberg, "Israeli tank blows up leading militant," *Guardian* (London), May 23, 2002; and Ferry Biedermann, "Secular but deadly: the rise of the Martyrs Brigades," March 19, 2002 at http://www.salon.com/news/feature/2002/03/19/brigades (accessed September 3, 2002).

[207] On November 27, 2001 in Afula, two Israelis were killed and fourteen wounded. Responsibility for the attack was jointly claimed by Islamic Jihad and al-Aqsa Martyrs' Brigades. The bat mitzvah attack in Hadera took place on January 17, 2002. Six civilians were killed and more than a dozen wounded.

Background

The links between Fatah and al-Aqsa are complex, yet ill-defined. Leaders and militants of the al-Aqsa Brigades have regularly identified themselves with Fatah. The al-Aqsa Martyrs' Brigades' letterhead carries the Fatah emblem, as do their websites, which also link to Fatah communiqués and documents. The al-Aqsa Brigades' martyrdom posters and statements of responsibility display both the al-Aqsa Martyrs' Brigades and Fatah emblems. According to documents captured by the IDF in April 2002 and made public, al-Aqsa Martyrs' Brigades members in 2001 requested funds from Fatah officials for personal, as well as military, support. (See section VII.)

Fatah leaders have frequently asserted that the organization never took a decision to set up the al-Aqsa Martyrs' Brigades or to recognize their claim to be the "military wing" of the organization. On the other hand, to our knowledge, neither individual Fatah leaders nor the ruling council of the organization have contested this claim or publicly dissociated Fatah from the al-Aqsa Martyrs' Brigades. Indeed, as noted above, in comments to a local newspaper in March 2002, West Bank Preventive Security chief Jibril Rajoub reportedly characterized the al-Aqsa Martyrs' Brigades as "the noblest phenomenon in the history of Fatah, because they restored the movement's honor and bolstered the political and security echelon of the Palestinian Authority."[208]

At the local level, many Fatah leaders have maintained an ambiguous relationship with the al-Aqsa Martyrs' Brigades. While not disavowing or disowning the al-Aqsa Brigades, most Fatah leaders have claimed that there is no supervisor-subordinate role between Fatah and al-Aqsa Martyrs' Brigades members, and that they have never exercised effective control over the al-Aqsa Martyrs' Brigades.

On several occasions since February 2002, Fatah leaders reportedly undertook efforts to end attacks on civilians by the al-Aqsa Brigades (see below). At the time of writing, al-Aqsa Martyrs' Brigades leaders had openly defied these efforts. In trial proceedings, Fatah leader Marwan Barghouti or others may provide more definitive answers concerning the degree, if any, of Fatah leaders' command responsibility for the grave violations of international humanitarian law committed by the al-Aqsa Martyrs' Brigades.

Involvement in Suicide Bombings

In many interviews, local Palestinian analysts and Fatah members told Human Rights Watch that the al-Aqsa Martyrs' Brigades undertook suicide

---

[208] Arieh O'Sullivan and Lamia Lahoud, "Rajoub praises Aksa Martyrs Brigades," *Jerusalem Post*, March 19, 2002.

bombings to counter growing public support for Hamas. (See above.) Although Fatah was always considered the pre-eminent PLO faction, its status and image suffered badly as a result of PA corruption and a widespread perception that it had lost the initiative to Hamas and Islamic Jihad in the struggle against Israel's military occupation. The al-Aqsa Martyrs' Brigades' first suicide bombing attack involved a tactic that guaranteed wide attention: the use of a female suicide bomber, Wafa' Idris. Since then, the al-Aqsa Brigades have explicitly differentiated themselves from Hamas and Islamic Jihad in their acceptance of female bombers. The al-Aqsa Brigades have also employed children: three of the perpetrators of al-Aqsa Brigades attacks in 2002 have been under the age of eighteen. (See below.)

The al-Aqsa Brigades' publicly justify their use of suicide bombings as the inevitable consequence of the sufferings of the Palestinian people. Ibrahim Abayat, leader of the al-Aqsa Brigades in the Bethlehem area, told an interviewer that attacks against civilians inside Israel "have come about as a result of the immense pressure endured by the Palestinian people lately.... These operations are completely unacceptable to us in al-Aqsa, but these operations do find some legitimacy when the occupation kills children and women in our camps in Jenin, Tulkarem, Nablus, Dheisheh...." When asked, "So, as a leader of the al-Aqsa Brigades, are you against suicide bombs?" Abayat was less categorical:

> The bottom line is that I am just one person among this Palestinian people. What generates vengefulness against the Israelis [is] the silence of the Israeli people in regard to the policies of Sharon.... There must be a message to the Israeli street: what is happening is not in your interest.[209]

Structure
The al-Aqsa Martyrs' Brigades describe themselves as being firmly in the lineage of other Fatah armed groups, such as "The Storm" (al-asifa) and the "Fatah Hawks."[210] In one document, posted on an al-Aqsa Brigades website, an

---

[209] Stuart Tanner, "Interviews with three Palestinian Militant Leaders," Battle for the Holy Land, PBS at http://www.pbs.org/wgbh/pages/frontline/shows/holy/onground/pales.html (accessed September 2, 2002). The interview was conducted on March 27, 2002, in preparation for a Frontline documentary, "Battle for the Holy Land," that first aired on April 4, 2002.

[210] See "The al-Aqsa Martyrs Brigades—Palestinian national liberation organization—Fatah", [Kata'ib Shuhada' al-Aqsa, haraka al-tahrir al-watani al-filastini] at

anonymous member describes the al-Aqsa Brigades' creation after the September 2000 visit of Ariel Sharon to the Temple Mount (*al-haram al-sharif*) in Jerusalem:

> At this point the Fatah movement got the long-awaited chance to adopt a new form and to continue the resistance of the persevering Palestinian people. A new phase has started to rise to the surface, with men who came with the sun like a storm, and who ran toward victory with the speed of leopards and the strength of falcons from afar in the sky of the nation. From here the al-Aqsa Brigades were formed in its different units in the southern and northern provinces of the nation [the West Bank and Gaza Strip]. And from there the National Resistance Committees and the Return (`awda) brigades were formed as an all-inclusive parameter for those sons of the nation and members of the Fatah movement who sought martyrdom.[211]

In an interview in the Lebanese weekly *al-Intiqad*, `Usama an-Najjar, identified as an "official spokesman" for the al-Aqsa Brigades, said their Brigades had been established "in the first month of the intifada" and that "its establishment was officially announced on January 1, 2001, during the military parade in commemoration of the establishment of the Fatah movement [January 1, 1965]. The al-Aqsa Brigades consider the killing of a Zionist settler near the West Bank village of Jalameh at the beginning of 2001 as its first operation."[212] Most of the al-Aqsa Brigades' important leaders appear to have come from the northern West Bank, and many have been captured, assassinated, or killed in clashes with the IDF.[213] Nasr Awais, Mahmud al-Titi, and Ra'id al-Karmi all openly acknowledged their role in the al-Aqsa Brigades prior to being captured or killed.

---

http://www.alaqsamartyres.org (accessed September 17, 2002). Translated by Human Rights Watch.

[211] Ibid.

[212] Excerpt and translation in "Statements by Heads of Fateh Factions," Special Dispatch Series no. 260, Middle East Media Research Institute (MEMRI), August 22, 2001.

[213] Israeli security forces have targeted individuals alleged to have planned or participated in attacks against Israeli military targets or civilians. Human Rights Watch has urged the Israeli authorities to end this practice. See Human Rights Watch press release and letter to then-Prime Minister Ehud Barak, "Israel: End 'Liquidations' of Palestinian suspects," January 29, 2001 at http://www.hrw.org/press/2001/01/ispr012901.htm.

Human Rights Watch field research, IDF documents, and Palestinian commentators all indicate that the al-Aqsa Brigades do not share the centralized decision-making character of Hamas or Islamic Jihad. "The Aqsa Brigades are ordinary people who identify with Fatah and are reacting to Israeli attacks," said `Awni al-Mashni, a member of the Fatah Higher Committee from Dheisheh refugee camp near Bethlehem and a critic of the militias. "Anyone could join and shoot at a settlement. Coordination emerged later."[214]

At least one ranking al-Aqsa Brigades cadre has asserted a direct link between the militias and the Fatah leadership. "Our group is an integral part of Fatah," said Maslama Thabet, identified as a 33-year-old al-Aqsa Brigades leader in Tulkarem. "The truth is, we are Fatah itself, but we don't operate under the name of Fatah. We are the armed wing of the organization. We receive our instructions from Fatah. Our commander is Yasir Arafat himself."[215] Asked about Thabet's assertion, Arafat spokesman Nabil Abu Rudeineh insisted, "The president has nothing to do with these things, he has nothing to say about this issue."[216]

Most observers, and al-Aqsa Brigades participants, disagree with Thabet's characterization.[217] According to "spokesman" `Usama an-Najjar: "The members of the al-Aqsa Martyrs are warriors who are not subject to any political decision and have no relation with the first rank of the PA, although some of its members work in sensitive positions in the PA's civil ministries or its security apparatuses.... The Brigades respect the national interest and choose the place and the time to carry out its operations." He characterized the Brigades as comprising "hundreds of members, aged between twenty-two and fifty-two, who were released from Israeli prisons or students in Palestinian universities who operate sometimes with and sometimes without coordination."[218]

Members of other armed groups agreed that the al-Aqsa Martyrs' Brigades are not a highly structured group. "Around here an Aqsa Brigade is any five or

---

[214] Human Rights Watch interview with `Awni al-Mashni, Dheisheh refugee camp, June 13, 2002.

[215] Matthew Kalman, "Terrorist says orders come from Arafat," *USA Today*, March 14, 2002.

[216] Ibid.

[217] Israel has made public a February 2002 memo ("memo to Tirawi") from the head of the PA's General Intelligence Services (GIS) in Tulkarem, which refers to Maslama Thabet as "an outcast" among the al-Aqsa Brigades fighters there. (The "memo to Tirawi" is analyzed in detail in section VII, below.)

[218] Excerpt and translation from interview in *al-Intiqad* in "Statements by Heads of Fateh Factions," Special Dispatch Series no. 260, MEMRI, August 22, 2001.

six guys who call themselves that," one PFLP member told Human Rights Watch in Jenin.[219] According to one high-level Western diplomat involved in security liaison between Israeli and Palestinian services, "there is no [al-Aqsa Brigades] infrastructure, just small groups making their own small decisions."[220]

These characterizations also conform to the statements of captured al-Aqsa Brigades members. `Abd al-Karim `Aweis, thirty-one, an al-Aqsa Brigades leader from Jenin refugee camp now in Israeli detention, told the *New York Times,* in an interview arranged by the Israeli internal security service, that the al-Aqsa Brigades' attacks were "organized at the local level, often in revenge for Israeli killings of suspected Palestinian militants, by volunteers who had let it be known that they were prepared to carry out suicide bombings or shootings."[221] Likewise, Lu'ay Shihab, an al-Aqsa Brigades member whose brother, Kamal Yusuf Shihab, was a middle-level al-Aqsa Brigades leader, told Human Rights Watch that Kamal would normally consult with Nablus and Balata camp-based al-Aqsa Brigades leaders Nasr `Awais or Mahmud al-Titi before initiating an attack, but that "in urgent circumstances he could decide on his own."[222]

The localized nature of the al-Aqsa Brigades' structure appears to be reinforced by a loose, personality-driven command structure. None of the more than twenty compilations of Palestinian documents publicly released by the IDF provide substantive evidence of any chain of military command between al-Aqsa groups and Arafat or other high-ranking PA and Fatah officials. One report of the PA General Intelligence Services (GIS), made public by the IDF, analyzes three different armed Fatah cells in Tulkarem, at least two of which were explicitly associated with the Brigades.[223] Comprising some twenty individuals in total, the groups described in the report appear to have opened contact with key Fatah and al-Aqsa Brigades figures on their own initiative, selecting one (or in the case of one group, several) patrons through whom they might channel requests for support. Members' relationships with Fatah appear to vary

---

[219] Human Rights Watch interview, name withheld, Jenin city, June 10, 2002.

[220] Human Rights Watch interview, name withheld, Jerusalem, June 6, 2002.

[221] Joel Greenberg, "Suicide planner expresses joy over his missions," *New York Times,* May 9, 2002.

[222] Human Rights Watch interview with Lu'ay Shihab, Nablus, June 8, 2002. `Awais was captured by Israeli forces during Operation Defensive Shield. Al-Titi was killed by an Israeli tank shell on May 22, 2002.

[223] "Document Eight: Excerpts from a Document of the General Intelligence Apparatus in the West Bank," IDF, April 4, 2002, TR1-248-02, at http://www.idf.il/english/announcements/2002/april/Fatah_Activists/10.stm (accessed September 4, 2002).

significantly, some close and reflecting deep involvement in internal power struggles, others remote.

Nasir Bardawi, an al-Aqsa Brigades commander from the Nablus area, told an interviewer in March 2002 that "there is no direct relationship at all" between the al-Aqsa Brigades and political leaders such as Yasir Arafat and Marwan Barghouti. But Bardawi also said that he considers the Brigades bound to obey any direct political order from the top to desist from armed attacks.[224] In a separate interview, however, Bardawi insisted that "al-Aqsa was not formed by a leadership decision, and it will not be dissolved by their decision."[225] The Brigades' reactions to Fatah attempts to dissolve them or bring their attacks on civilians to an end, described below, lend credence to this second characterization.

The role of Marwan Barghouti, Fatah's general secretary in the West Bank, is highly controversial. Israeli officials allege that Barghouti functioned as the head of the al-Aqsa Brigades until his arrest in April 2002. On August 14, 2002, Israel's Justice Ministry indicted him in the Tel Aviv District Court on charges that he is "the founder" of the al-Aqsa Brigades and that he used funds "from different sources both inside and outside Israel," including from the PA, "to finance many activities carried out by terror cells in the West Bank."[226]

Barghouti has not acknowledged that he played such a role, but documents made public by Israel indicate that, at a minimum, Barghouti functioned as a patron on behalf of several al-Aqsa Brigades groups, referring requests for individual financial assistance to Yasir Arafat. One well-informed Nablus-based Palestinian journalist told Human Rights Watch that Barghouti was "very popular and highly respected" in the area. "He was the struggle face of Fatah, but his main means of communication was interviews on Jazeera television," this person said. "When he said 'the intifada will continue' he was expressing policy, not just his opinion. But he resisted local al-Aqsa Brigades efforts to

---

[224] Ferry Biedermann, "Secular but deadly: the rise of the Martyrs Brigades," March 19, 2002 at http://www.salon.com/news/feature/2002/03/19/brigades (accessed September 4, 2002).

[225] Tim Cornwell, "If he wants to be a suicide bomber, he comes to us," *The Scotsman*, March 9, 2002. Nasir Bardawi is identified in this interview as "Yasser" Badawi.

[226] According to an IDF Spokesman, August 15, 2002, the indictment charges that "the accused … led the terrorist organizations in Judea and Samaria, and as such played a central role in all their decision making processes. The accused was subordinate to Yasser Arafat, who is the recognized head of all of these terrorist organizations." See also "The State of Israel versus Marwan Ben Hatib Barghouti," IDF, August 14, 2002 at http://www.idf.il/english/ishumim/bargouti.stm (accessed September 3, 2002).

engage him in helping to set their agendas."[227] Human Rights Watch will examine evidence of the allegations against Barghouti and other militants made public in any trials that may be held.

Fatah leaders have repeatedly insisted that the military elements responsible for the attacks are not under the control of the political leadership. For example, Hussein al-Sheikh, a Fatah political leader who has frequently spoken supportively of the Brigades in the media, told Human Rights Watch, "I am against touching civilians.... I will tell you an important thing: not all military acts by al-Aqsa were done with the agreement of the political wing."[228]

Muhammad `Abd al-Nabi, a Fatah leader from the Dheisheh refugee camp, noted that for many in the al-Aqsa Brigades, their professed identity with Fatah did not necessarily translate into compliance with Fatah decisions, such as the late May announcement of Fatah's Central Committee calling for a halt to attacks inside Israel and the disbanding of the militias. "So someone records a cassette and says he's Fatah—we can't object to this," `Abd al-Nabi told Human Rights Watch. "He's a hero in the community. In the community the Central Committee doesn't count for much."[229] Hussam Khader, a member of the Fatah Higher Committee from Balata refugee camp, decried suicide bombing attacks on civilians in an interview with Human Rights Watch but estimated that "[the bombings] have about 80 percent support." "But leaders are supposed to lead," he said. "The problem is the big gap between us and the traditional leadership. The new generations don't respect them. There is no Fatah—only people who call themselves Fatah."[230]

The disjuncture between official Fatah statements and the Brigades' actions have been particularly clear on the several occasions on which Fatah leaders have attempted to shut down the Brigades. For example, on February 7, 2002, the Fatah leadership in Ramallah reportedly held a secret meeting in which it decided to dissolve the Brigades. A statement issued in the name of the Brigades in Gaza accepted the decision, but a second statement, faxed from the

---

[227] Human Rights Watch interview, name withheld, Nablus, June 7, 2002. One al-Aqsa Brigades statement at the time the IDF launched Operation Defensive Shield referred to the Brigades as being "under the leadership of Marwan Barghuti." "Al-Aqsa Bridages call for unity, name Barghuti as leader for first time," Agence France-Presse, April 1, 2002.

[228] Human Rights Watch interview with Hussein al-Sheikh, Ramallah, May 14, 2002.

[229] Human Rights Watch interview with Muhammad `Abd al-Nabi, Dheisheh refugee camp, June 12, 2002.

[230] Human Rights Watch interview with Hussam Khader, Balata refugee camp, June 7, 2002.

West Bank, rejected it. "We denounce those who want to create confusion by announcing the dissolution of the Brigades," the statement said. "We remain faithful to the blood of our martyrs and will continue our operations."[231]   In news reports on Arabic and Islamist websites, al-Aqsa Brigades leaders were widely quoted as saying that the Brigades had not been founded by the decision of any official organization or group—and they could not be disbanded by them, either.[232]

In late March 2002, Nasr `Awais, by all accounts one of the leaders of the al-Aqsa Brigades in the northern West Bank, issued a leaflet in which he proclaimed himself the overall head of the al-Aqsa Brigades, and declared that, notwithstanding President Arafat's declarations of a cease-fire, the al-Aqsa Martyrs' Brigades "is continuing in the path of ...armed resistance.... We will compete with each other over who will become a martyr first."[233] "President Arafat himself cannot ask us to accept being slaughtered by Israel like sheep without defending ourselves," `Awais said in an interview. "They are continuing their occupation and, therefore, we will keep up the fight." `Awais asserted that the al-Aqsa Brigades "aim only at their soldiers, but when they kill our civilians we can do nothing but respond."[234]

Palestinian and Israeli analysts told Human Rights Watch that some al-Aqsa Martyrs' Brigades adherents in the northern West Bank may also get some financial support from Munir Muqdah, a Fatah leader in the `Ain al-Hilweh refugee camp in Lebanon, further complicating Arafat's limited influence in that region. Muqdah broke with Arafat in 1993 to protest the Oslo Accords, and is reputed to have close relations with Hizbollah, Iran, and Syria. In late May 2002, the Israeli daily *Ha'aretz*, citing Shin Bet sources, reported that captured Brigades leader Nasr `Awais told interrogators that Muqdah had provided him with between $40,000 and $50,000 over the previous year for arms and explosives, and that the two spoke on a weekly basis.[235] A *Jerusalem Post* report in August 2002 quoted an unnamed Fatah official as saying that Muqdah used

---

[231] "Fatah Splinter Group Denies Plans to Dissolve," Agence France-Presse, February 12, 2002.

[232] See for example, "Al-Aqsa Brigades Dissolved," (in Arabic) al-Jazeera February 12 2002 at http://www.aljzeera.net/news/arabic/2002/2/2-12-3.htm (accessed June 5, 2002). Translated by Human Rights Watch.

[233] Mohammed Daraghmeh, "Palestinian militia linked to Arafat's Fatah says it will keep up attacks," Associated Press, March 22, 2002.

[234] Nidal al-Mughrabi and Steve Weizman, "Palestinian militia won't halt attacks," *Ottawa Citizen*, March 23, 2001.

[235] "Shin Bet: Lebanon Fatah man tied to Tanzim hits," *Ha'aretz*, May 27, 2002.

funds from Syria and Iran "to undermine the local Fatah leadership and establish his own bases of power here," naming Jenin, Tulkarem, and Nablus.[236]

In May 2002, *al-Hayat* reported that the 130-member Fatah Revolutionary Council issued a statement condemning "military operations inside Israel...because they are likely to have a negative impact on national resistance."[237] But Fatah cadres later insisted the statement had not been issued. `Ali Mahbul, the Fatah secretary-general for the Nablus district, discussing the May 2002 draft statement in an interview with Human Rights Watch, said that the Fatah leadership had "discussed how to control reactions" of the al-Aqsa Brigades to Israeli attacks. "One suggestion is that Fatah leaders be assigned to monitor and control" the actions of the Brigades, "but the decision was not taken. We are still discussing it—very difficult and sensitive."[238]

On August 12, 2002, responding to Fatah-led efforts to negotiate a joint platform of all factions on a halt to attacks against civilians inside Israel and a publicly declared moratorium on such attacks by Fatah, the al-Aqsa Brigades reportedly declared that it would in fact continue such attacks "unless Israel withdraws from the Palestinian territories, releases Palestinian prisoners and stops assassinating Palestinian leaders."[239] The same dynamic was repeated in mid-September 2002, when the text of a Fatah statement rejecting all attacks against civilians was leaked to the Israeli press—and sharply criticized by al-Aqsa leaders in the northern West Bank.[240] At the time of writing, Fatah had not yet taken any concrete steps to disassociate itself from the al-Aqsa Martyrs' Brigades or to apply political pressure to bring an end to the Brigades' attacks on civilians. `Awni al-Mashni gave the view of many local Fatah leaders who have criticized suicide bombings against civilians when he told Human Rights Watch that implementing any initiative such as that considered in May by the

---

[236] Khaled Abu Toameh, "New Fatah groups controlled by PLO dissident in Lebanon," *Jerusalem Post*, August 26, 2002. The article also says that Muqdah supported the Battalions of Return, which it characterized as a "Fatah breakaway group."

[237] "Revolutionary Council and DFLP call for an end to attacks inside Israel," *al-Hayat*, May 30, 2002 (in Arabic). The statement reportedly followed "two weeks of internal debate" and was to be distributed to the eleven groups that constitute the PLO.

[238] Human Rights Watch interview with Ali Mahbul, Nablus, June 8, 2002.

[239] Graham Usher, "Cease-fires that cannot be," *Middle East International*.

[240] "Fatah Armed Wing Denies Cease-fire Reports, Vows to Continue Armed Struggle," text of Israel radio report, BBC Monitoring Middle East, September 10, 2002.

Fatah Revolutionary Council would not be possible without some form of Israeli reciprocity. "Fatah may say stop," he said, "but no one will listen."[241]

In sum, the al-Aqsa Martyrs' Brigades' command structure appears to be locally centered, but effective. The al-Aqsa Brigades members refrained from— or were incapable of—carrying out suicide bombings against civilians from November 2000 to January 2002. From January onward, the al-Aqsa Martyrs' Brigades' actions heralded a sharp increase in the frequency of suicide attacks. Al-Aqsa Brigades members who planned or participated in such attacks are individually criminally responsible for their actions; their local leaders can be held responsible both directly and, for attacks perpetrated by their local subordinates, under the doctrine of command responsibility. Based on currently available evidence, however, Human Rights Watch did not find that Fatah officials possessed a supervisor-subordinate relationship over the al-Aqsa Martyrs' Brigades or the effective control required to hold the Fatah leadership criminally liable for the actions of the Brigades.

Popular Front for the liberation of Palestine (PFLP)

The Popular Front for the Liberation of Palestine (PFLP), once a professedly Marxist alternative to mainstream Palestinian nationalist groups, has its roots in the Arab National Movement (ANM). The ANM was set up in Beirut, Lebanon, in 1948, following the first Arab-Israeli war and the establishment of the state of Israel. The first secretary-general of the ANM, George Habash, established the Popular Front for the Liberation of Palestine in 1967—following the second Arab-Israeli war—and was elected as the first PFLP secretary-general. The PFLP gained notoriety in the late 1960s and early 1970s for its role in commercial airline hijackings.

Background

The PFLP opposed the Madrid and Oslo peace processes and suspended its participation in the PLO for several years following the signing in 1993 of the Declaration of Principles between Israel and the PLO. Habash stepped down for health reasons in July 2000 and was succeeded by Abu `Ali Mustafa, a founder and former commander in chief of the PFLP military forces, and deputy secretary-general since 1972. The PFLP had sought to have Mustafa based in the Palestinian-controlled areas, and Israel allowed him to return to the PA territories in October 1999, following a reconciliation between the PFLP and the PLO.

---

[241] Human Rights Watch interview with 'Awni al-Mashni, Dheisheh refugee camp, June 13, 2002.

During the current clashes, the PFLP has claimed responsibility for three suicide bombing attacks on civilians as well as car bombings, which reportedly injured several dozen civilians. In August 2001, Mustafa was killed by an Israel missile attack on his West bank office.[242] He was succeeded by Ahmad Sa'adat as secretary-general and `Abd al-Rahim Malluh as deputy secretary-general. The PA detained Sa'adat on January 15, 2002, after he was reportedly lured to a hotel meeting with West Bank Palestinian intelligence chief Tawfiq Tirawi. He is currently detained in Jericho under U.S. and U.K. supervision.[243] The IDF detained Malluh in mid-June 2002.

The PFLP has in the past called for the "liberation" of all of historic Palestine. The group's most recent platform, however, enunciated at its sixth national congress on July 7, 2000, continues to reject the Oslo Accords and later agreements between the PLO and Israel but accepts that "new realities have been created since Oslo that cannot be ignored: the emergence of the Palestinian Authority (PA) and the retreat of Israeli soldiers from ten Palestinian cities."[244] It calls for the establishment of a Palestinian state with Jerusalem as its capital, withdrawal of Israeli soldiers to the 1967 borders, the dismantling of Israeli settlements, and the right of return for Palestinian refugees.[245]

Involvement in Suicide Bombings
In the context of the current clashes, the PFLP rose to prominence in October 2001 after its military wing, the Abu `Ali Mustafa Brigades, assassinated the Israeli Minister for Tourism, Rehavam Ze'evi, on October 17. Prior to this attack, the PFLP took responsibility for five car bombings,

---

[242] The U.S. government condemned the missile attack because the office was located in a building inhabited by civilians, and Israel's policy of targeted killings was "an excessive use of force and unhelpful to efforts to quiet the ongoing violence." Kenneth Katzman, "Terrorism: Near Eastern Groups and State Sponsors, 2002," *CRS Report for Congress*, Library of Congress Congressional Research Service, February 13, 2002, p. 24 at http://www.fas.org/irp/crs/RL31119.pdf (accessed September 3, 2002).

[243] In early June the Palestinian High Court in Gaza ruled that Sa'adat should be released because of the "absence of any charges leveled against him." See Fathi Sabah, "Israel threatens action if Sa'adat is released," *al-Hayat*, June 4, 2002. The Palestinian cabinet refused in response to threats by Israeli leaders that, in Prime Minister Sharon's words, "we will bring justice to him" if he were released. See Suzanne Goldenberg, "Palestinians ignore court call to free faction leader," *Guardian* (London), June 4, 2002.

[244] PFLP press release, "The Popular Front for the Liberation of Palestine Finishes its Sixth National Conference," July 7, 2000 at http://www.pflp-pal.org/press/conferences.html (accessed September 3, 2002).

[245] Ibid.

including four in Jerusalem within seven hours on September 4, 2001, in which nine people were injured.[246]

As of the end of August 2002, the PFLP had claimed responsibility for three suicide bombing attacks against civilians. On February 16, 2002, a suicide bomber blew himself up in a shopping mall in the West Bank settlement of Karnei Shomron, killing three teenagers and injuring around thirty. The attack was claimed by the Abu `Ali Mustafa Brigades of the PFLP in a statement announcing that the bomber, Sadiq `Abd al-Hafiz, had come from the West Bank town of Qalqiliya. The second attack, injuring fifteen people, targeted the lobby of a hotel on the outskirts of the Ariel settlement on March 7. In the third attack, on May 19, the suicide bomber disguised himself as an Israeli soldier and blew himself up at a Netanya open-air market, killing three and wounding fifty-nine. Hamas also claimed responsibility for this attack.

Structure

The PFLP has not claimed any separation between its military wing and its political leaders. As with the other armed Palestinian groups that have intentionally and repeatedly organized suicide attacks against civilians, persons carrying out attacks on civilians claimed by the PFLP are individually criminally liable for their actions. PFLP leaders are also liable both directly and under the doctrine of command responsibility.

Recruitment and Use of Children

The Palestinian Authority has endorsed international mechanisms that prohibit the use of children under the age of eighteen in hostilities. In April 2001, it sent a delegation to a regional conference on the use of child soldiers; the conference adopted a resolution declaring that "the use in hostilities of any child under eighteen years of age by any armed force or armed group is unacceptable."[247] On May 9, 2002, the PA addressed the United Nations Special Session on Children and advocated the application of the Optional Protocol to the Convention on the Rights of the Child, which prohibits the recruitment or use in hostilities of those under the age of eighteen.[248]

---

[246] Matthew Levitt and Ehud Waldoks, "The Return Of Palestinian Nationalist Terrorism," *Peacewatch,* no. 379, May 3, 2002 at http://www.washingtoninstitute.org/watch/Peacewatch/peacewatch2002/379.htm (accessed September 3, 2002).

[247] Amman Declaration on the Use of Children as Soldiers, April 10, 2001.

[248] Statement of Dr. Emile Jarjou'i, Head of Delegation of the Observer Delegation of Palestine on the occasion of the Special Session of the General Assembly on Children, May 9, 2002 at http://www.un.org/ga/children/palestineE.htm (accessed June 6, 2002).

Most perpetrators of suicide bombing attacks have been young men aged eighteen to twenty-four. At least three bombings, however, have been carried out by children—persons under the age of eighteen. At least two have been from the Bethlehem area, and all three attacks were claimed by the al-Aqsa Martyrs' Brigades. Muhammad Daraghmeh, age seventeen, killed himself and five other children when he carried out a suicide attack for the al-Aqsa Brigades on March 2, 2002, in an orthodox neighborhood of Jerusalem (eleven civilians were killed and almost fifty wounded). In another al-Aqsa Brigades attack in a park in Rishon Letzion on May 22, 2002, `Issa Bdeir, age sixteen, killed two civilians and injured at least twenty-four. The third child bomber was Majd `Atta, seventeen, who killed himself and injured five others in an attack on a falafel shop in central Jerusalem on July 30, 2002.

On June 28, 2002, an Israeli military court sentenced a sixteen-year-old boy to life imprisonment after he was apprehended in an attempt to blow himself up on or near a bus. At his sentencing, the boy said he had been "deceived" by Hamas into participating in the unsuccessful attack.[249] Islamic Jihad acknowledged that to perpetrate a bombing on June 9, 2002 at Megiddo Junction, its members taught Hamza Samudi to drive; his age has been given variously as sixteen, seventeen, and nineteen.[250]

The participation, acknowledgment, and acceptance of the use of children to perpetrate suicide bombings have continued despite widespread Palestinian unease with such tactics. This unease intensified in April 2002 following three separate incidents in the Gaza Strip in which several Palestinian boys between the ages of fourteen and sixteen were killed as they charged the perimeter of an Israeli settlement armed with knives and crude pipe bombs.

By all accounts, no Palestinian group organized or sponsored these would-be attacks. Nevertheless, both Hamas and Islamic Jihad felt pressure to respond to a popular sense that the promotion of "martyrdom operations" had encouraged young people to participate in them. On April 24, the Palestinian Legislative Council "express[ed] its worry and disapproval toward this phenomenon as well as its refusal to accept its continuation" and "call[ed] on all

---

[249] Amos Harel, "Failed suicide bomber, sixteen, sentenced to life in prison," *Ha'aretz*, June 28, 2002.

[250] Brennan Linsley, "Car Bomber Just Learned to Drive," Associated Press, June 6, 2002.

bodies and sectors related to this phenomenon to stop this trend in order to protect our children and their right to life."[251]

Hamas and Islamic Jihad both later disavowed the use of children. A Hamas statement, also on April 24, referring to the incidents as "a dangerous trend," called on mosque imams "to give this issue some mention in their sermons" and on educators "to dedicate time to address this issue without sacrificing the enthusiasm or spirit of martyrdom of our youth [*ashbaluna*]."[252] An Islamic Jihad communiqué of April 26, citing Islamic strictures against the participation of children in war, declared: "We refuse any encouragement given to young people that might drive them to act alone or be pushed by others into action. They are not ready and not able to do so." The statement called on "mothers, fathers, teachers, political leaders and presidents to work closely with, and advise children, on what will assist them and …their communities to cope. Encourage them to concentrate on and complete their education, allow them to express their enthusiasm by participating in public demonstrations…and prepare them to face the enemy once they are adults."[253] However, neither group indicated a minimum age for recruitment, and the Arabic terms used do not rule out the use of children under the age of eighteen in military activities.

The al-Aqsa Brigades have not formally addressed the issue of employing children in armed actions but media reports indicate awareness of the matter among activists. One account, based on interviews with al-Aqsa Brigades and other militias in Nablus, reported that "the factions say that suicide volunteers under the age of eighteen are rejected."[254] An al-Aqsa Brigades fighter named Fayez Jaber told a reporter that age was among the group's criteria for choosing volunteers. "A person has to be a fully matured person, an adult, a sane person, and of course, not less than eighteen years of age and fully aware of what he is about to carry out," Jaber said.[255]

Such disavowals mischaracterize the use of children, as if the decision to carry out a suicide bombing were an entirely voluntary and independent act that

---

[251] The statement, referring to a council meeting of April 21, was issued by the office of the Speaker of the Legislative Council on the letterhead of the Palestinian National Authority.

[252] Access to this statement at http://www.qassam.org/hamas/bayanat/24_04_2002 is currently blocked. Translated by Human Rights Watch.

[253] Islamic Jihad communiqué, "Protect our children from being killed," April 26, 2002. Translated by UNICEF, Jerusalem.

[254] Paul McGeough, "Guided Missiles," *Sydney Morning Herald*, April 13, 2002.

[255] Gregg Zoroya, "Her decision to be a suicide bomber," *USA Today*, April 22, 2002.

does not need logistical support, supplies, training, and other assistance from a sponsoring organization. The May 22 Rishon Letzion bombing and the June 9 Megiddo bombing were committed after these disavowals and criticisms of children's participation. The May 22 attack was carried out by `Issa Bdeir at sixteen; the youngest suicide bomber to date. The al-Aqsa Brigades and Islamic Jihad claimed responsibility for those respective attacks.

Some Hamas leaders have been more forthright about their readiness to recruit children to participate in hostilities. In a "discussion" posted on the `Izz al-Din al-Qassam Brigades website, Salah Shehadah, the late leader of the militia, was asked how he dealt with the "phenomenon" of "young boys [shabab] seeking martyrdom without approaching any of the military agencies." He replied, "It is an indicator of the positive consciousness of Palestinian society and not a fault.... If some young people are not abiding with the regulations of the military agency and were not officially linked to it, this is proof that the nation of Islam [umma] has become a jihadist umma that refuses disrespect and oppression...." Shehadah goes on to say, that "this trend...could be misused" and that "there is a need to instruct those children [al-ashbal] in a special military section that gives them a jihadist military education so that they can distinguish right from wrong and know when they are capable of carrying out a martyrdom operation and when they should not."[256]

There have been several reports of segments on PA television that explicitly encourage children to take part in clashes with Israeli forces and extol the virtues of martyrdom.[257] In recent months, lively discussion about the effects of such programming on children has taken place in the Palestinian community.[258]

On August 26, 2002, the Palestinian Journalists Syndicate called on Palestinian armed factions to stop using children, and declared that it was "absolutely forbidden" for photojournalists to take pictures of children carrying weapons or taking part in militant activities. The statement said that footage of armed children served "the interests of Israel and its propaganda against the Palestinian people." Tawfiq Abu Khousa, deputy chair of the syndicate, said, "We have decided to forbid taking any footage of armed children, because we

---

[256] See http://www.qassam.net/chat/salah3.html (accessed August 8, 2002). Translated by Human Rights Watch.

[257] "The Anatomy of Child Self-Sacrifice" was a video shown on Palestinian Media Watch, July 2001 at http://www.pmw.org.il, though it is no longer available.

[258] Ashraf al-Ajrami, "Why Palestinian Children Become Martyrs," al-Ayyam, May 6, 2002.

consider that as a clear violation of the rights of children and for negative effects these pictures have on the Palestinian people."[259]

It is the encouragement of children to carry weapons and take part in armed activity that is wrong, not media coverage of these activities. The PA has publicly endorsed the Convention on the Rights of the Child and has urged respect for the provisions of the Optional Protocol to the CRC on Involvement of Children in Armed Conflict.[260] The PA should take steps to prevent the recruitment and use of persons under eighteen years of age in hostilities. These steps should include adoption of legal measures to prohibit and criminalize such practices, a public education campaign to ensure that this policy is widely communicated, and measures to ensure that materials produced with PA funding, or media outlets supported by PA funding, do not encourage children to participate in military activities.

---

[259] "Palestinian group warns journalists," Associated Press, August 26, 2002.

[260] Statement of Dr. Emile Jarjou'i, Special Session of the General Assembly on Children, May 9, 2002. In 2001, the PA participated in a regional conference on child soldiers that resulted in the Amman Declaration that says participants "solemnly declare that the use in hostilities of any child under 18 years of age by any armed force or armed group is unacceptable." See Amman Declaration on the Use of Children as Soldiers, April 10, 2001.

VI. FINANCIAL AND LOGISTICAL SUPPORT

Under international law, those who assist, aid, or abet crimes against humanity are individually responsible for the resulting crimes. Both governmental and private organizations have provided financial and logistical support to groups responsible for suicide attacks against civilians. Others have given funds to groups that may have been diverted to fund such activities, or, through the provision of large cash payments to perpetrators' families, have rewarded those who carried out such attacks. This section discusses the varying means by which regional governments and other entities have tangibly supported suicide bombings.

Funding Overview of Perpetrator Groups

Several governments, notably the United States and Israel, have asserted that Hamas receives funding for armed activities and logistical support from governments in the region, including Iran and Syria. Hamas has also received extensive support for its social programs and military activities from individuals and charitable foundations in Saudi Arabia, other countries in the Gulf area, the United States, and elsewhere. One recent press report cites Israeli intelligence experts as saying that Hamas's annual operational income "tops at least $20 million a year."[261] Although exact figures are not known, a considerable portion of Hamas's resources are devoted to charitable and social programs. A Western diplomat based in the region and familiar with Palestinian political organizations told Human Rights Watch that the proportion of Hamas finances devoted to armed activities "represents a small portion of their resources." [262] Asked about reports of state funding of Hamas, the group's spokesman, Ismail Abu Shanab, told Human Rights Watch that the organization gets no financial support from "formal sources," and that this was one expression of the group's "independence."[263]

In contrast to Hamas's complex and varied financial structure, Islamic Jihad is generally thought to derive almost all its funding from state sponsors, particularly Iran. According to the U.S. State Department, Islamic Jihad receives financial assistance from Iran and "limited logistical support assistance" from

---

[261] Larry Kaplow, "Backgrounder: Israel's Adversaries: Hamas: Back-seat driver to Arafat group; Palestinian-run movement opposes the peace process," *Atlanta Journal-Constitution,* January 24, 2002.

[262] Human Rights Watch interview, name withheld, Jerusalem, June 6, 2002.

[263] Human Rights Watch interview with Ismail Abu Shanab, Gaza City, May 15, 2002.

Syria.[264] According to the Israeli government, documents captured by the IDF in PA offices in April 2002 indicate that Islamic Jihad received "massive financial aid" from the group's headquarters in Damascus, but documents supporting this assertion have not been made public.[265] One publicly available document, a report from the Palestinian National Security Forces in Jenin to the West Bank head of the PA General Intelligence Services (GIS), Tawfiq Tirawi, states that Islamic Jihad operatives in Jenin received funds via bank transfer from Ramadan Shalah, the Islamic Jihad secretary-general in Damascus, but does not indicate the amount of money thus transferred.[266] The transfers included financial assistance for the families of Islamic Jihad members in prison or killed, as well as support for Islamic Jihad military operations.

The al-Aqsa Martyrs' Brigades appear to have benefited from the routine misuse of PA funds. Arafat and other senior PA officials, as well as many rank-and-file Fatah members, have overlapping identities as employees or officials of the PA, on the one hand, and as members of Fatah on the other. This dual identity appears to have facilitated the use of PA resources to fund Fatah activities directly and indirectly, including payments to individual al-Aqsa Brigades activists (discussed in Section VII). Yet the al-Aqsa Brigades appear to have had more limited resources than Hamas or Islamic Jihad, at least in the northern West Bank. Kamal Yusuf Shihab, a mid-level al-Aqsa Brigades militant in Nablus, received no salary or stipend as a militant and continued to work as a mechanic. "He worked his job during the day and was a militant at night," his brother told Human Rights Watch.[267] `Ata Abu Rumaila, a Fatah leader in Jenin refugee camp, told Human Rights Watch that militants there received "no support" from the PA and that weapons had been "bought out of our own pockets."[268] In one captured document, on the letterhead of the al-Aqsa Martyrs' Brigades in Jenin governorate and addressed to Fatah secretary-general Marwan Barghouti, the writer complained, "At the same time the Islamic factions receive all the financial aid they require for working and for purchasing

---

[264] U.S. Department of State, *Patterns of Global Terrorism 2001*, Appendix B, May 15, 2002, p. 103.

[265] See IDF report, "Jenin: The Capital of Suicide Terrorists," circa April 19, 2002 at http://www.idf.il/english/news/jenin.stm (accessed September 3, 2002).

[266] "Cooperation between Fatah and the PA Security Apparatuses with Islamic Jihad and Hamas in the Jenin Area", IDF, April 9, 2002 at http://www.idf.il/jenin/site/english/main_index.stm (accessed September 3, 2002).

[267] Human Rights Watch interview with Lu'ay Shihab, Nablus, June 8, 2002.

[268] Human Rights Watch interview with `Ata Abu Rumaila, Jenin refugee camp, June 11, 2002.

arms. They recruit boys with motivation in that they supply them with arms, give them a monthly salary, and solve all their economic problems."[269] This situation, at least in the Jenin area, may have led to financial assistance from the local Islamic Jihad group to al-Aqsa Martyrs' Brigades.[270] No action or authorization is indicated on the document.

Little is known about funding of the PFLP. Like Islamic Jihad and Hamas, it has a headquarters in Damascus. According to the U.S. State Department, the PFLP receives logistical and safe haven assistance from Syria, and has training facilities in Syrian-controlled areas of Lebanon. One U.S. government analyst told Human Rights Watch that the high-profile killing of the Israeli minister of tourism in September 2001 had enabled the PFLP to attract new external sources of support, but provided no details.[271]

State Support for Suicide Attacks Against Civilians

Iran

Perhaps the most frequently cited example of state support for suicide attacks against civilians are the money and training that Iran provides to Hamas and Islamic Jihad. The U.S. government has attributed Iran's support for armed activities to two institutions: the Revolutionary Guard Corps and the Ministry of Intelligence and Security. Both institutions are accountable only to Iran's Supreme Leader, Ayatollah Khamenei. Iranian officials have routinely denied such allegations of support.[272]

---

[269] See Document A, the letter dated September 25, 2001 in IDF report, "Jenin: The Capital of the Palestinian Suicide Terrorists," p.16.

[270] On the lack of funding, see IDF Document 8, "The Al-Aqsa Martyrs Brigades and Fatah Organization are One and the Same.... [F]ragment of a letter allegedly from the Fatah movement in Jenin Refugee Camp to Marwan Barghouti," September 25, 2001; IDF Document 9, "Report on letterhead of the al-Aqsa Brigades of Jenin governorate to Marwan Barghouti," 8 May 2001; "Letter from Khaled `Abd-al Azia Muhammad Sif to Marwan Barghouti," (undated); and IDF Document 3, "Additional Captured Documents Reveal Again the System of Money Transfers to Terrorist Squads, Personally Authorized by Yasser Arafat, with the Deep Involvement of Marwan Barghouti," IDF, June 24, 2002, TR6-498-02. For the allegation that Islamic Jihad gave financial support to the al-Aqsa Brigades, see "February 4, 2002 report to the head of Palestinian General Intelligence from Abu Aziz " in "The Cooperation Between Fatah and the PA Security Apparatuses with PIJ and Hamas in the Jenin Area," IDF, April 9, 2002 TR3-268-02, p. 15.

[271] Human Rights Watch interview, name withheld, Washington, DC, June 12, 2002.

[272] The charge has also come from PA officials. Haidar Irshaid, the acting governor of Jenin, when asked about sources of support for Islamic Jihad in his district, told Human Rights Watch that he was "not authorized to say" but that he had "heard" that the group

Few details are available publicly about this assistance, and accounts vary widely. Islamic Jihad's relationship with Iran is anchored in the organization's ideological affinity with the pan-Islamic revolutionary program of the Ayatollah Khomeini. Israeli analyst Meir Hatina dates the organization's "material dependence on Iran" to Israel's expulsion of Islamic Jihad founders Fathi `Abd al-`Aziz al-Shikaki and Suliman `Awda to Lebanon in 1988.[273] In 1995, al-Shikaki said Iranian support was "very limited." "The Islamic Republic of Iran supports the Palestinians politically and morally," he told correspondent Robert Fisk. "Our organization gets some support for the families of martyrs."[274] In 1996, Ambassador Philip Wilcox, then the Coordinator for Counter-terrorism in the U.S. State Department, said that Iran's assistance to Islamic Jihad was at that time some two million dollars per year.[275]

Reports regarding Iranian funding of Hamas vary widely. An IDF report from January 1993 stated that "Hamas receives financial support from unofficial bodies in Saudi Arabia and the Gulf states, and recently also from Iran."[276] A recent report by the Congressional Research Service of the U.S. Library of Congress, citing the State Department, estimated that total Iranian funding for Hamas represented approximately 10 percent of the organization's budget but

---

received support from Iran and Syria. Human Rights Watch interview with Haidar Irshaid, Jenin city, June 10, 2002. In 1999, Police Chief Gazi al-Jabali claimed that the PA had evidence showing Iranian transfers of million of dollars to Hamas for the purpose of influencing the Israeli elections, a charge Iranian officials contested. Ibrahim Barzak, "Police chief: Hamas plans attacks to help Netanyahu win election," Associated Press, February 4, 1999. More recently, but without naming funders or organizations, President Arafat said, "[T]he orders to carry out these actions come from extremist organizations outside Palestine. They are also financed from outside Palestine," BBC Monitoring Middle East cited Palestinian Television, "Arafat says extremist organizations receive orders, financing from abroad," June 30, 2002.

[273] Hatina, *Islam and Salvation in Palestine*, pp. 41, 108. Hatina writes that Iranian financial and logistical aid was "disbursed through the Iranian Embassy in Beirut and through Hizballah," p. 108.

[274] Robert Fisk, "The Doctor who Finds Death a Laughing Matter," *The Independent* (London), January 30, 1995.

[275] Wilcox's statement, made to Stephen Flatow and his lawyer in July 1996, was cited in the findings of a U.S. court judgment in a suit for monetary damages that Flatow brought against Iranian officials as a result of the death his daughter, Alicia Flatow, in a suicide bombing in April 1995. See *Flatow v. Iran: Order*, filed on March 11, 1998 at http://www.ict.org.il/counter_ter/law/lawdet.cfm?lawid+16 (accessed August 16, 2002).

[276] IDF Spokesman, "HAMAS – The Islamic Resistance Movement," January 1993, p. 10 at http://www.fas.org/irp/world/para/docs/930100 (accessed August 16, 2002). The document also estimates that the funds reaching Hamas "operatives" in the West Bank and Gaza Strip annually amount to around $1 million.

did not provide an estimate of the dollar size of Hamas's budget or the amount of Iran's contribution.[277] As noted above, Israeli intelligence experts have estimated the annual operational budget of Hamas as being at least $20 million.

Iran has also reportedly provided training and other forms of support to Hamas. In a recently published interview, Hassan Salameh, a Hamas member from Gaza serving forty-six consecutive life sentences in Israel for his role in the 1996 suicide bombings, said that after he fled to Sudan via Jordan in 1993, "the organization arranged a training camp for us and flew us to Syria and then to Iran."[278] In June 2002, the regional press reported high-level meetings of Iranian, Hamas and Islamic Jihad officials in Iran, and noted that Iranian authorities had decided to increase the financial aid given to Hamas and Islamic Jihad. According to one report, the Iranians were also considering a "special budget for backing some Palestinian figures whose organizations lost their financial sources after the collapse of the Soviet Union," possibly referring to the PFLP.[279] Islamic Jihad leaders were reportedly promised a 70 percent increase in funding and told that it would pass to them directly, rather than via Hizbollah in Lebanon.[280]

The U.S. government contends that the Iranian government has been encouraging greater coordination of Islamic Jihad and Hamas with Hizbollah.[281] Israeli intelligence reports state that Hamas receives training and access to explosives from Hizbollah, and funding from Iran via the Hamas office in Damascus, which is headed by Musa Abu Marzuq and Khalid Mish'al.[282] Asked in June 2001 about allegations of Hamas collaboration with Hizbollah, Shaikh

---

[277] See Kenneth Katzman, "Terrorism: Near Eastern Groups and State Sponsors, 2002," p. 7, *CRS Report for Congress,* Library of Congress Congressional Research Service, February 13, 2002 at http://www.fas.org/irp/crs/RL31119.pdf (accessed September 3, 2002). The report says that Hamas funding comes "from businesses it runs in Palestinian controlled areas, from Iran (about 10% of its budget), from wealthy private benefactors in the Persian Gulf monarchies, and Palestinian expatriates." It does not provide any estimate of the size of Hamas' budget.

[278] Post and Sprinzak, "Terror's Aftermath," *Los Angeles Times,* July 7, 2002.

[279] Ali Nurizadeh, "Iran Increases budget to Islamic Jihad and special assistance to resistance leaders," *Al-Sharq al-Awsat,* June 8, 2002 (in Arabic).

[280] Ibid.

[281] U.S. Department of State, Office of the Coordinator for Counterterrorism, *Patterns of Global Terrorism 2000,* April 30, 2001 at http://www.state.gov/s/ct/rls/pgtrpt/2000/2441.htm (accessed September 3, 2002).

[282] For an account of a Tehran meeting of Hamas and Hizbollah leaders, see Matt Rees, "The Terror Twins," *Time,* April 30, 2001.

Yassin responded, "It is our right to cooperation with any side that serves our cause, whether Hizbollah or others."[283]

Syria
Syria provides safe haven as well as logistical support, and serves as a conduit for funds, to several groups that perpetrate suicide attacks against civilians. Islamic Jihad, Hamas, and the PFLP all have headquarters or a high-level presence in Damascus. Islamic Jihad and Hamas also have "basing privileges" for training and other activities in the Beka'a Valley, an area of Lebanon under effective Syrian control.[284] Both Islamic Jihad and the PFLP are said to have received financial support from Syria in 1998, although there is little public evidence of Syrian financial contributions to armed activities since then.[285] In late September 2002, Syria reportedly rejected U.S. efforts to include specific mention of Hamas and Islamic Jihad in a draft U.N. Security Council resolution. Each had claimed responsibility for suicide bombings in Israel the week before, which were to be mentioned in the draft.[286]

A memorandum from the PA Preventive Security office in Bethlehem to the PSS Central Operations directorate, dated May 1, 2000 and made public by the IDF, forwards second-hand information from a PSS informant asserting that Islamic Jihad funding in the Bethlehem area comes from Damascus through Amman to the Cairo-Amman Bank in Palestine, and that a second stream comes from Saudi Arabia through Cairo to the same bank. This memo reports that

---

[283] Interview, *al-Mujalla*, translated in Foreign Broadcast Information Service (FBIS), Near East and South Asia, June 17, 2001.

[284] U.S. Department of State, *Patterns of Global Terrorism 2000.*

[285] See Katzmann, "Terrorism: Middle Eastern Groups and State Sponsors, 1999", p. 17. On funding via Syria, see "Perpetrator of hotel attack in Netanya was disguised as a Woman," *Yediot Ahronot* (in Arabic) May 16, 2002. Translated by Human Rights Watch. The article reflects the purported admissions under Israeli interrogation of Abbas al-Sayid, a Hamas leader from Tulkarem, arrested on or about May 6, 2002. According to the article, "Al-Sayid testified that he was used to contacting Hamas leadership in Syria when he needed money, and he used to receive $10,000 - $13,000 each month. These monies were deposited in his personal account and the account of his wife. He said that he was aware the source of the money was Europe and the U.S. as it was clear from the bank statements."

[286] Julia Preston, "Israel resists new U.N. measure to end siege," *New York Times*, September 25, 2002. Syria is currently a member of the Security Council.

funds are transferred monthly but to individuals whose identities change "according to conditions."[287]

Syria has consistently refused to take steps to limits its assistance to armed Palestinian groups that perpetrate suicide attacks. It claims that such groups are engaged in legitimate resistance against occupation but makes no effort to disassociate itself from attacks on civilians, in clear violation of international humanitarian law.[288]

Iraq

The government of Iraq has expressly endorsed and encouraged suicide bombing attacks against civilians. Iraq, in its provision of funds to families of "martyrs" and others, has established a differential in which families of suicide bombing operatives are said to receive a considerably larger sum of $25,000, while other families that have suffered a death receive $10,000.[289] In promoting suicide attacks, Iraqi leaders have made no distinction between attacks against civilians and attacks against military targets.

Iraq provides these monies through the local Ba'th Party-affiliated Arab Liberation Front (ALF). The ALF is a constituent member of the Palestine Liberation Organization, and a representative sits on the PLO executive committee, but it is not considered to have a significant number of adherents and is not credited with playing any role in the current clashes other than as a conduit for Iraqi government funds and propaganda. The ALF has told reporters that Iraq has provided $20 million in aid to Palestinians since clashes began in September 2000, but it is not known what portion of that amount has been provided to families of suicide bombers.[290] One Gaza-based ALF official, Ibrahim al-Za'anin, told Reuters, "President Saddam made clear that [suicide] attacks must be considered the utmost act of martyrdom."[291]

---

[287] "Analysis of the Captured Documents: The Saudi Committee for the Support of Intifada al Quds," Appendix D, from http://www.idf.il/ (accessed July 2, 2002). The informant's source reports that she does not know the names of recipients. Reports or allegations of Saudi support for Islamic Jihad are uncommon.

[288] See Syria's report to the U.N. Security Council on measures taken to implement UN Security Council Resolution 1373. U.N. Document S/2001/1204, December 14, 2001.

[289] Iraq increased its payment of $10,000 to "martyrs'" families to $25,000 in the case of suicide bombers in March 2002.

[290] Sky TV broadcast of July 17, 2002, shotlist and storyline provided to Human Rights Watch by Associated Press Television News, August 7, 2002.

[291] Nidal al-Mughrabi, "Iraqi, Saudi aid money wins Palestinian hearts," Reuters, June 2, 2002.

There are several accounts of public events where such payments have been made. Reporter Paul McGeough described a meeting of some 200 members of forty-seven families who gathered in the Tulkarem chamber of commerce in March 2002 to collect checks.[292] Two were families of suicide bombers. ALF secretary-general Rakad Salem told McGeough in Ramallah that as of late March 2002 more than eight hundred families of Palestinians killed in the unrest had received $10,000 "martyr" payments, and that the funds had been "transferred by the banks—from the Iraqi banks to the banks in Palestine."[293] The Tulkarem ALF officials told McGeough that the additional $15,000 payment was to encourage more volunteers for suicide missions.[294] A member of the Palestine Legislative Council was reportedly among those presiding at the Tulkarem event.

Another report described an ALF gathering on May 20 in the Gaza Strip at which forty-six families of "martyrs" received $10,000 apiece and the families of two suicide bombers received $25,000 apiece.[295] In a Sky TV broadcast of a similar event staged by the ALF in Gaza on July 17, 2002, members of families of "martyrs" killed in the violence received certificates and $10,000 checks, while families of suicide bombers received $25,000.[296] The report did not indicate the numbers of families in either category.

Other Forms of Funding or Support

In addition to funding from governments, Hamas receives funding from individual benefactors and charities, some in the Persian Gulf region and others in the Palestinian and Arab diaspora in the United States, Europe, and elsewhere. In Saudi Arabia, some of the charities that solicit funds for Palestinian charities allegedly associated with Hamas do so under royal

---

[292] Paul McGeough, "A sea of blood…a sip of coffee," *Sydney Morning Herald*, March 26, 2002. Some details of the meeting are from McGeough's letter of April 6, 2002, posted on the website of the Campaign Against Sanctions in Iraq, www.casi.org.uk/discuss/2002/msg00517 (accessed August 7, 2002).

[293] Paul McGeough, "Saddam Stokes War With Suicide Bomber Cash," *Sydney Morning Herald*, March 26, 2002. Israelli forces reportedly arrested Salem in early October 2002. "Israel says arrests pro-Iraq leader in W. Bank," Reuters, October 2, 2002.

[294] Paul McGeough, letter of April 6, 2002, was posted on the website of the Campaign Against Sanctions in Iraq, http://www.casi.org.uk/.

[295] Nidal al-Mughrabi, "Iraqi, Saudi aid money wins Palestinian hearts," Reuters, June 2, 2002.

[296] Shotlist, soundbite and storyline provided to Human Rights Watch by Associate Press Television News.

patronage. The U.S.-based Holy Land Foundation for Relief and Development, which the U.S. government forcibly closed in December 2001 on the grounds that it was a Hamas front organization, reportedly listed revenues of $13 million on its tax returns for the year 2000, and allegedly channeled funds to Hamas through local charity committees in the West Bank and Gaza.[297] One Bahamas-based financial institution, al-Taqwa Bank, is alleged to have been the repository of some $60 million in Hamas-related funding for the year 1997 alone.[298]

The U.S. and Israeli governments allege, and Hamas denies, that these funds "leak" to the organization's armed wing.[299] Examples of Hamas-controlled societies that allegedly received funds from the Holy Land Foundation were the Islamic Charitable Society of Hebron, the Jenin Zakat Committee, and the Ramallah Zakat Committee, each of which had among its officials persons who had allegedly admitted to armed activities with Hamas, including attacks against civilians.[300] U.S. authorities have also cited Israel's interrogation of Muhammad Anati, former head the Foundation's Jerusalem Office, in which Anati reportedly confessed that funds intended for charitable use were diverted to Hamas's military activities.[301]

Hamas enjoys a reputation for financial probity, in contrast to the reputed corruption of the PA, and its network of welfare activities, associated with local

---

[297] Matthew A. Levitt, "Charitable and humanitarian Organizations in the Network of International Terrorist Financing," testimony before the Subcommittee on International Trade and Finance, Committee on Banking, Housing and Urban Affairs, August 1, 2002, p. 4. Officials of the Holy Land Foundation have denied providing support for military activities.

[298] Testimony of Juan C. Zarate, Deputy Assistant Secretary for Terrorism and Violent Crime, US Department of the Treasury, House Financial Subcommittee, Oversight and Investigations, February 12 2002, PO-1009 at http://www.ustreas.gov/press/releases/po1009.htm (accessed September 3, 2002).

[299] The EU has held the position that separation between Hamas military and charitable activities is possible, and has banned fundraising on behalf of the Hamas military wing, the `Izz al-Din al-Qassam Brigades. See "Decision Adopted by Written Procedure, Fight Against Terrorism – Updated List," Brussels 3 May 2002, 8549/02 (Presse 121) at http://ue.eu.int/Newsroom (accessed September 3, 2002).

[300] "Summary of Information Provided by the FBI to the Department of Treasury in Support of the Designation of the Holy Land Foundation for Relief and Development," no date, provided to Human Rights Watch by the U.S. Department of Justice, August 2002.

[301] United States District Court for the District of Columbia, *Holy Land Foundation for Relief and Development v. John Ashcroft in his official capacity as Attorney General of the United States*, Civil Action no. 02-442 (GK), Memorandum Opinion & Order filed August 8, 2002 by Judge Gladys Kessler, p. 29.

Muslim charity organizations, is in many areas reportedly more extensive than those of the PA. IDF analysts, commenting on documents captured from Palestinian offices, wrote, "it can be assumed that some of funds that were transferred to the Hamas or entities linked to it also trickled to the Hamas operational-military apparatus," but the IDF made no information public to support this assertion.[302] The U.S. government has also argued that Hamas's charitable activities provide a benign cover through which funds can be transferred from abroad into Hamas-controlled institutions.[303]

However, Ziad Abu `Amr, a Gaza-based independent member of the Palestine Legislative Council, told Human Rights Watch that he has examined the books of large Hamas-affiliated charities in Gaza in his capacity as chair of the PLC Political Committee. "One of the Hamas groups that Arafat closed in December [2001] was the Islah [reform] Society, which is big money," he said. "We examined their books carefully. There was nothing amiss. I went to Arafat and said, on what basis are you shutting them down?" Abu `Amr said that funding for Hamas's military activities may well come from outside states such as Iran but that he is convinced that social and charitable funds are kept separate. "They will not jeopardize their social institutions," he said. "That is their strength, their existence."[304]

Whether or not funds intended for charitable purposes are diverted to the Hamas military wing, Hamas spokespersons openly acknowledge that the group sees its sizeable social programs as a means of building and maintaining popular support for its overall political goals and programs, including its militant and armed activities. "The political level is the face of Hamas, but without the other divisions Hamas would not be as strong as it is now," spokesperson Ismail Abu Shanab told a reporter. "So it needs the three parts to survive. If nobody supports these needy families, maybe nobody would think of martyrdom and the resistance of occupation."[305] Another Hamas leader, Ibrahim al-Yazuri, in an interview in a Hamas-affiliated magazine, characterized Hamas's objective as "the liberation of all Palestine from the tyrannical Israeli occupation" "This is

---

[302] See IDF captured documents, "Saudi Arabia Finances Terror Activities; Strengthening the Hamas' attack apparatus," www.idf.il/saudi_arabia/site/english (accessed October 4, 2002).

[303] U.S. Department of Justice brief, *Holy Land Foundation v. John Ashcroft,* p. 4 section I (A).

[304] Human Rights Watch interview, Washington, June 28, 2002.

[305] Megan Goldin, "Hamas feeds struggle against Israel with charity," Reuters, January 4, 2001.

the main part of its concern," he said. "Social work is carried out in support of this aim."[306]

Payments to Family Members of Those Who Carry Out Attacks Against Civilians.

Many of the organizations that donate to Hamas-related or other charitable groups provide compensation support to families of "martyrs"—generally defined as individuals who have been killed, disabled or imprisoned during the current clashes. A significant portion of the funding to the charities and other organizations that provide these programs appears to come through non-governmental channels from Saudi Arabia and other countries, with government approval. In the case of Iraq, funding comes directly from the government (see above). Human Rights Watch is not aware of any effort by the PA to restrict payments from reaching families of suicide bombers who have attacked civilians.

Israeli authorities have publicized a figure of some $33,000, made up of payments from Iraq, Saudi Arabia, the PA, Qatar, and the United Arab Emirates that it says goes to families of suicide bombers.[307] Human Rights Watch could not confirm that payments of such scale with any regularity. Palestinians interviewed by Human Rights Watch agreed that families of "martyrs" generally received financial assistance, but said that, except in the case of Iraqi payments, such funds were provided to families of all persons whose death was related to confrontations with Israeli forces, not only to those who carry out suicide attacks.[308]

Among the PA documents captured by the IDF in April-May 2002 are records relating to payments from the Saudi Arabian Committee for Support of the Intifada al-Quds, headed by the Saudi Arabian Interior Minister, to the

---

[306] The interview in *Filastin al-Muslimah* (no date cited) is translated and excerpted in "Summary of Information Provided by the FBI to the Department of Treasury in Support of the Designation of the Holy Land Foundation for Relief and Development," no date, provided to Human Rights Watch by the U.S. Department of the Treasury, August 2002.

[307] IDF Captured Document "Saudi Arabia Finances Terror Activities", Appendix F at http://www.idf.il/saudi_arabia/site/english/main_index.stm (accessed September 3, 2002).

[308] Only one out of the seven families of perpetrators visited by Human Rights Watch in the preparation of this report acknowledged receiving any financial assistance from any outside quarter—in that case, a check for seventy dollars from the United Arab Emirates.

Tulkarem Charity Committee.[309] Under the arrangement, all payments or distributions were made on the basis of information supplied by "Palestinian elements," and were arranged through some fourteen local charity committees, many of which had links to Hamas.[310] Each charity committee made payments or distributed food to the needy, and also gave both lump-sum and ongoing payments to families of individuals killed, injured, or imprisoned in the intifada, including the families of individuals from Hamas or other armed groups who had carried out suicide attacks against civilians.[311] The PA strenuously objected on the grounds that it was designed to undercut its authority, but not because the payments were rewarding attacks on civilians.

Palestinians for the most part support the provision of assistance to families that have lost loved ones, and do not believe that families of perpetrators of attacks against civilians should be denied such assistance. "I myself am deeply opposed to suicide bombings, yet I too support the families," the prominent Gaza-based psychiatrist and human rights activist Eyad Sarraj said in a recent interview. "As a Palestinian, as an Arab, as a Muslim, and as a human being ...I cannot leave their children in poverty—I have to do what I can to leave them some hope and dignity. This is why we support the families— certainly not to encourage suicide bombing."[312]

However, as discussed in Section III, individuals who die in the course of committing a crime against humanity should not be equated with individuals who are victims of attacks or who die in ordinary combat. In the case of Iraq's payment of a sizeable "premium" to families of suicide bombers, the intent is expressly to encourage the commission of crimes against humanity. Such

---

[309] IDF captured documents, "Saudi Arabia Finances Terror Activities" at http://www.idf.il/saudi_arabia/site/english/main_index.stm (accessed September 3, 2002).

[310] "Many of the *zakat* committees may not be controlled by Hamas, but they are under the influence of the Muslim Brothers more broadly," one well-informed Palestinian journalist told Human Rights Watch, referring to the Islamist political group from which Hamas emerged. "Individuals and religious societies in Saudi Arabia will get names and account numbers from an organization like the Hebron Charitable Society." Human Rights Watch interview, name withheld, Nablus, June 7, 2002.

[311] IDF captured documents, "Saudi Arabia Finances Terror Activities" at http://www.idf.il/saudi_arabia/site/english/main_index.stm (accessed September 3, 2002).

[312] Interview with Eyad Sarraj, "Suicide Bombers: Dignity, Despair, and the Need for Hope," *Journal of Palestine Studies* XXXI, no. 4 (Summer 2002), p. 75.

payments should be stopped.[313] In the view of Human Rights Watch, the family of a person responsible for carrying out suicide attacks against civilians should be eligible for financial assistance only as part of a general welfare program based on demonstrated financial need. The provision of funding to the families of individuals who perpetrate suicide attacks against civilians in any other circumstances is wrong. Even payments that do not privilege the families of suicide bombers should not be made to such families in any manner that confers social honor, such as a status of "martyr" or war victim, on the persons responsible for carrying out crimes against humanity.

The PA Ministry of Social Affairs says that it provides a small monthly sum to the family of any person killed or injured in confrontations with Israeli forces or settlers. Yusuf Abu Laban, head of the Bethlehem office of the ministry's Committee to Care for Martyrs' Families, told Human Rights Watch that the amount depends on whether the victim was a primary breadwinner, and the family's economic circumstances. Laban also indicated that the committee plays a role in coordinating the distribution of some funds contributed from elsewhere. Outside contributions, he said, also come to the locally based Islamic Development Bank, "which has a list of eligible martyr families." In other cases, he said, such as funds from Iraq, the sums go directly to the families. Laban insisted that the PA ministry gives no preference or special treatment whatsoever to the families of suicide bombers. "We are first of all a social assistance agency, and we provide only if the family needs it."[314] However, the PA makes no apparent effort to limit special payments by others to the families of suicide bombers who attack civilians.

Local charitable societies also provide financial assistance. Shaikh Ahmad al-Kurd, the Hamas-affiliated Islah (reform) Society in Gaza, of which he is the president, was quoted in the Saudi press as saying that the society provided $5,300 to families of persons killed or disabled in the conflict, $1,300 to injured persons, $2,650 to families whose homes have been destroyed or badly damaged, and $2,600 to families of prisoners.[315] Shaikh Ahmad gave no indication that people who attacked civilians were excluded from this policy.

---

[313] For example, life insurance policies typically preclude payment when the deceased has taken his or her own life, so as not to provide any incentive to committing suicide. The rationale behind the above exclusion is all the stronger if the suicide is committed in the course of perpetrating a crime against humanity.

[314] Human Rights Watch interview with Yusuf Abu Laban, Bethlehem, June 13, 2002.

[315] Fahem al-Hamid and 'Abdul Qadir Faris, "Saudi society distributes relief aid to Palestinians in Gaza," *Saudi Gazette*, May 2, 2002. The Shaikh said that in Gaza there were 518 martyrs' families and 4,027 injured persons.

Some news reports indicate that Hamas has provided additional "compensation" to the families of suicide bombers.[316]

Media reports as well as reports of government intelligence agencies indicate that compensation provided to Palestinian families who have had a member wounded, imprisoned, or killed during the current clashes has to a considerable extent been funded from foreign sources. One example is the Saudi Committee for Support of Intifada al-Quds, mentioned above. Of some 102 names listed in the committee's tenth cycle of payments to the Tulkarem Charity Committee, at least ten were individuals responsible for ordering or condoning attacks against civilians during the current clashes. One example is the payment made to the family of `Abd al-Rahman Muhammad Said Hmaid, who was allegedly involved in the suicide attack on the Dolphinarium discotheque on June 1, 2001.[317]   Payments were also made to the families of perpetrators of suicide attacks against civilians in 1995-96. According to an IDF analysis (originals were of too low a quality to permit independent examination), information on each victim included the cause of death, with those who had carried out suicide attacks clearly marked. The committee should cease payments to the families of individuals who have committed crimes against humanity.

Under international law, governments and private organizations incur criminal liability for assisting groups or individuals to carry out suicide bombings against civilians. No support should go to any organization that continues to commit such crimes against humanity. If a group is engaged in parallel legitimate activities, such as charitable welfare, no funds should be provided until a verifiable scheme is established to ensure that no funds are diverted for criminal purposes. In no case should individuals or their families be privileged in any payment because of participation in attacks that target civilians. Governments have an obligation to investigate and prosecute any individual or entity within their jurisdiction that violates these standards.

---

[316] Amanda Ripley, "Why Suicide Bombing....Is Now All The Rage," *Time*, April 15, 2002. Ripley reported that "[a]t wakes for Hamas bombers, it has become routine for an activist to approach the father with an envelope containing $10,000."

[317] The scanned Arabic originals released by the IDF were of too poor a quality to allow analysis.

VII. THE ROLE OF THE PALESTINIAN AUTHORITY

One of the most contested questions in the debate about Palestinian suicide attacks on Israeli civilians is what, if any, role has been played by the Palestinian Authority and specifically, President Arafat. Israel charges that the PA has ordered and systematically participated in "terror," a term it applies to all armed activity against Israeli targets, whether military or civilian. It holds the PA responsible every time an attack occurs. The PA denies having any role in attacks against civilians.

The PA, under the terms of the Oslo Accords, assumed law enforcement responsibilities for those areas of the West Bank and Gaza Strip under its control—namely, the major cities and Palestinian population clusters, amounting at the time of the outbreak of clashes in September 2000 to approximately 26 percent of the West Bank and 60 percent of the Gaza Strip.[318] The PA thus has had an obligation to take all available and effective measures consistent with international human rights and humanitarian law to prevent suicide or other attacks against civilians by the armed groups operating from these areas.

Human Rights Watch found that there were steps that the PA could have taken to prevent or deter such attacks, but that it remained unwilling to risk the political cost of acting decisively. The PA routinely failed to investigate, arrest and prosecute persons believed to be responsible for these attacks, and did not take credible steps to reprimand, discipline, or bring to justice those members of its own security services who, in violation of declared PA policy, participated in such attacks. In addition, although President Arafat repeatedly condemned suicide attacks against civilians, he consistently failed to insist that terms of honor and respect such as "martyr"—which Palestinians use to designate persons who have died or suffered grave loss in clashes with Israeli forces or settlers—should not apply to people who die in the course of carrying out indiscriminate attacks against civilians.

Moreover, President Arafat and other senior officials authorized payments, in several cases, to individuals who were known to have participated in attacks on Israeli civilians in the Occupied Territories and, more commonly, without apparent regard for the known or alleged involvement of the recipients in attacks on civilians. As discussed above, President Arafat and the PA also took no steps to ensure that welfare payments from the PA and others did not privilege the families of suicide bombers who attacked civilians. Indeed, one document made

---

[318] Of the 26 percent of the West Bank under PA security control, the PA shared joint security responsibility with Israel for 23 percent, and 3 percent was under its sole control. Beinin, J. "The Demise of the Oslo Process", March 26, 1999. MERIP PIN no. 1 at http://www.merip.org/pins/pin1.html (accessed October 10, 2002).

public by the Israeli government, hereafter referred to as the "memo to Tirawi," suggests that at least one senior PA intelligence official may have had a positive view of people who carry out attacks on civilians.[319]

The PA's failure to act in an effective and consistent manner against Palestinian attacks on civilians contributed to an atmosphere of impunity, allowing the armed groups to conclude that there would be no serious consequence for those who planned or carried out attacks that amounted to war crimes, and in the cases of suicide bombings, crimes against humanity. This failure reflects a high degree of political responsibility on the part of President Arafat and the PA leadership for the many civilian deaths that have resulted.

However, on the basis of evidence available through the end of September, 2002, Human Rights Watch did not find evidence demonstrating that President Arafat or other senior PA officials ordered, planned, or carried out suicide bombings or other attacks against civilians. While senior PA officials fostered an atmosphere of impunity, we also did not find evidence that they authorized specific attacks or attacks against civilians generally, or that PA officials or institutions organized or assisted in preparing or carrying out attacks against civilians systematically or as a matter of policy. The "memo to Tirawi" suggests that at least some senior PA officials viewed these attacks favorably, but, as discussed in Section V, the PA and the Fatah political leadership did not have the effective control over the actions of the al-Aqsa Martyrs' Brigades necessary to establish criminal liability under the doctrine of command responsibility.

Security Role of the PA Since September 2000

The Oslo process required that one of the central functions of the Palestinian Authority was to maintain law and order, prevent armed attacks against Israelis or Israeli targets, and bring to justice those accused of perpetrating such attacks. Some Palestinian armed groups rejected the Oslo agreement because, among other things, it was preconditioned on renouncing armed resistance against Israeli occupation.

While the post-Oslo negotiations continued, there was a significant level of cooperation between Israeli and Palestinian security forces, particularly in the aftermath of a suicide bombing campaign perpetrated by Hamas and Islamic Jihad in 1996-97. During this period, by most accounts, the PA took credible

---

[319] See the report to Tawfiq Tirawi, head of the General Intelligence Services (GIS) in the West Bank, from Hamdi Darduk, the GIS head in Tulkarem, entitled "The General Situation Among Armed Fatah Personnel in the District," February 6, 2002.

and tangible steps to prevent attacks against Israeli targets.[320] Ely Karmon, an Israeli counter-terrorism analyst, commenting on the decline in attacks by Hamas and Islamic Jihad in this period, wrote that it "was due to the combined preventive counter-terrorist policy of the PA and Israel."[321] Yoram Schweitzer, another Israeli analyst, noted as an example of this cooperation a March 2000 Hamas attempt to carry out attacks in Israeli cities that was thwarted by the capture of two of the leaders in Nablus by Palestinian forces.[322] A senior official in the West Bank Preventive Security Service told Human Rights Watch, "1999-2000 were the best years ever from a security standpoint. When it worked we had help from Israelis—people like [former Shin Bet chief] Ami Ayalon, [former IDF chief-of-staff Lieutenant General Amnon] Shahak, [former Justice Minister Yossi] Beilin, the old [Shimon] Peres."[323] Ramadan Shalah, secretary-general of Islamic Jihad, appeared to confirm this assessment regarding his organization. "The Oslo agreement," he wrote in March 2002, "demolished the foundations of the Palestinian resistance.... The Islamic movement entered a period of crisis that had more or less led to the breakdown of its military infrastructure, where it had lost most of its human and financial resources."[324]

With the deterioration of Israeli-Palestinian political relations and the onset of the current unrest, cooperation between Israeli and PA security forces diminished rapidly. From the outset, Israeli authorities accused the Palestinian Authority, and President Arafat personally, of being directly responsible for attacks against Israelis. For example, after a roadside bomb killed two civilians

---

[320] For an account of how security cooperation fared in response to the suicide bombings in early 1996, see James Bruce, "The PLO, Israel and Security," *Jane's Intelligence Review,* April 1, 1996. For a critique of PA human rights abuses in its arrest and treatment of detainees in this period, see Human Rights Watch, "Human rights under the Palestinian Authority," *A Human Rights Watch Report,* vol. 9, no. 10 (E), September 1997.

[321] Karmon, "Hamas' Terrorism Strategy...," *Middle East Review of International Affairs,* p. 66.

[322] Yoram Schweitzer, "Suicide Terrorism: Development and Characteristics," lecture presented in the International Conference on Countering Suicide Terrorism at ICT, Herzeliya, Israel, February 21, 2000 at http://www.ict.org.il/ (accessed October 10, 2002).

[323] Interview, name withheld, Jerusalem, June 9, 2002.

[324] Shalah goes on to write that the Hizbollah victory over the IDF in southern Lebanon and the collapse of the July 2000 Camp David talks "opened a new window of opportunity for the Palestinian people to return to the option of intifada and resistance." "The Islamic Jihad movement in Palestine: Preliminary Remarks," (in Arabic) *Al-Intiqad* (weekly) no. 924, March 2002.

and seriously wounded nine others, including five children, in an armored school bus passing near the Kfar Darom settlement in the Gaza Strip on November 20, 2000, then-Prime Minister Ehud Barak blamed Arafat and Fatah and in retaliation ordered IDF helicopters and naval vessels to shell PA and Fatah headquarters and Preventive Security Services (PSS) offices in Gaza City.[325] Many Palestinians, for their part, blamed the PA for not protecting them from attacks by the IDF and Israeli settlers in the Occupied Territories.

Mutual recriminations continued, and violence intensified. On the Palestinian side, the stoning of IDF checkpoints gave way to roadside shootings of civilians and military targets and, finally, to suicide bombing and shooting attacks against civilians as well as military targets. On the Israeli side, continuing instances of indiscriminate and/or excessive use of force were aggravated by increasingly severe restrictions on freedom of movement, a policy of assassinations of alleged militants, frequent raids into PA-controlled areas, and, finally, full-scale military re-occupation of those areas.

As the spiral of violence wound tighter, the Palestinian Authority continued to condemn publicly armed attacks that deliberately targeted civilians but, except for a brief period from mid-December 2001 to mid-January 2002, took no clear or credible actions to prevent such attacks or to punish those responsible. The PA's inaction was at least in part due to its unwillingness to confront the organizations carrying out such attacks, which enjoyed a high degree of popular Palestinian support, particularly in light of mounting Palestinian civilian casualties.

The main PA security agency responsible for enforcing PA commitments to combat anti-Israeli violence is the Preventive Security Service. With separate commands in the Gaza Strip and the West Bank, the PSS at its height numbered between four and five thousand officers, mostly former Fatah fighters. Some PSS officers were trained by the U.S. Central Intelligence Agency. [326] Few observers, however, would characterize it as a professional law enforcement agency.[327] Along with the General Intelligence Service (GIS) and other PA

---

[325] Arafat condemned the roadside bomb attack, for which no group claimed responsibility.

[326] For an overview of this relationship, see "The Palestinian Authority and the CIA," *IISS [International Institute for Strategic Studies] Strategic Comments,* vol. 4, no. 10, December 1998.

[327] One independent Palestinian analyst, asked by Human Rights Watch about links between Fatah and the al-Aqsa Martyrs' Brigades, said that the Brigades were "freelance Fatah" while the PSS was "the real armed wing of Fatah," with a mission of enforcing PA (i.e., Fatah) policy vis-à-vis the Islamist opposition Human Rights Watch interview, Washington, D.C., September 4, 2002.

security forces, the PSS served as a kind of job bank for the Palestinian leader, in addition to performing policing, intelligence, and coercive functions.

The PA's failure to take effective steps to prevent suicide attacks against civilians and bring those responsible to justice dates from the earliest months of the current unrest. However, as clashes continued and intensified, Israeli attacks targeting Palestinian security services infrastructure, places of detention, and security personnel, along with curfews and stringent restrictions on movement, gradually undermined the PA's enforcement capabilities.

These attacks were generally carried out as retaliation for Palestinian attacks on Israeli targets. For example, on May 18, 2001, following a Hamas suicide bombing in Netanya that killed five and injured more than 100, Israel attacked PA security installations in Gaza City, Nablus, Ramallah, and Tulkarem. In Nablus, F-16 warplanes bombed the main prison complex, killing eleven policemen.[328] In an interview in late December 2001, Preventive Security Services chief Jibril Rajoub said that more than 70 percent of its offices and 90 percent of its barracks had been destroyed.[329] Israeli military analyst Gal Luft wrote, in the aftermath of Operation Defensive Shield, "The IDF has targeted PSS installations in its retaliatory attacks against Palestinian terrorism, destroying almost every PSS headquarters, office, training base, and vehicle."[330] Many Israelis as well as Palestinians saw in these attacks an Israeli government policy aimed at weakening the PA to the point of collapse. On July 17, 2002, after a suicide bombing in Tel Aviv, Minister for Public Security Uzi Landau said, "We will enter their areas and break up the entire Palestinian security apparatus to bring about the collapse of the Palestinian Authority."[331]

On September 4, 2002, meeting with Danish Foreign Minister Per Stig Moeller, President Arafat said that Palestinians are "able to fully control the

---

[328] On May 20, 2001, an IDF tank shelled the home of Colonel Jibril Rajoub, West Bank head of the PSS. Rajoub was at home at the time but escaped harm. The IDF later said that it was responding to shooting from a position nearby and had been unaware of the fact that it was Rajoub's home, but the officer in command of the tank unit told a radio interviewer that his men knew who they were targeting. See the *Economist*, May 26-June 1, 2001, pp. 43-44.

[329] "Palestinian Security Chief on Cease-fire Decision, Compliance of Hamas," *Al-Musawwar* (Cairo), December 28, 2001, excerpts translated by Foreign Broadcast Information Service (FBIS), Near East and South Asia, document number: FBIS-NES-2002-0102.

[330] Gal Luft, "Reforming the Palestinian Security Services," The Washington Institute for Near East Policy, *Peacewatch*, no. 382, May 15, 2002.

[331] "Pair of Bombers Strike in Tel Aviv, Killing Three in Street," *New York Times*, July 18, 2002.

security situation" in the areas of PA jurisdiction.[332] Speaking a day earlier, however, and reflecting a less optimistic assessment shared by many outside observers as well, PA Interior Minister `Abd al-Razaq Yahya told Reuters that the PA security services were "facing great difficulty" in regaining control of the security situation.[333]

Failure to Bring to Justice those who Ordered, Planned, or Participated in Suicide Attacks on Civilians

Although the PA's legal governing authority derives from the Oslo Accords signed with Israel, the duty to prevent systematic indiscriminate attacks against civilians is not contingent on Israeli compliance with those accords or rendered null by what the PA regards as Israeli violations of the accords. That duty should not be a bargaining chip whose implementation is subject to political negotiations. As the political authority in place, the PA has a responsibility to bring to justice individuals who order, plan, or carry out attacks against civilians. The PA has failed to meet this obligation.

When the PA made arrests, they were often indiscriminate, picking up supporters of one or another militant group without regard to any alleged responsibility for the serious crimes being committed in the name of that group. Instead of being investigated, detained suspects were typically held without charge and later released. The PA has explained these releases as a response to the danger posed by Israeli bombings of places of detention, but it has not tried to explain why suspects were not investigated, charged, or brought to trial.

PA officials also claim that Israeli actions, such as the destruction of PA police and security installations, have undermined the PA's capacity to act. However, the record indicates that the PA for the most part did not attempt to exercise its capacity to prevent or punish such crimes even when it had the ability to do so. At least until the IDF's reoccupation of Palestinian cities and towns in April 2002, the PA retained some degree of law enforcement capacity. In June 2001, and again in mid-December 2001, the PA showed that it still commanded enough influence with the perpetrator groups, using political negotiations as well as coercive law enforcement measures, to bring about cessations of suicide bombings, even though its law enforcement capacities had been diminished by Israeli attacks.

The relative success of the PA's intervention with armed groups and their sponsors in the December 2001-January 2002 period highlights the PA's lack of

---

[332] "Arafat says he accepts EU peace plan 'in principle'," *Ha'aretz* (September 4, 2002).

[333] Mark Heinrich, "Militants endanger security deal—Israeli general," Reuters, September 3, 2002.

similar concerted effort at other times, in particular during the violent months that preceded the December 2001 initiative. This failure to take consistent and credible steps to confront these attacks contributed to a climate of impunity and set the scene for the escalation of such attacks between late January and early April of 2002.

In the first weeks of the clashes, the PA released numerous detainees, most of them members of Hamas and Islamic Jihad, some of whom had been in PA detention without charge or trial for several years.[334] According to press reports, the first releases took place on October 4, 2000, when twelve Hamas detainees were released from Gaza Central Prison. Subsequent releases occurred over the following week. A PA security official in Gaza claimed that by mid-October the PA had "begun to re-arrest them."[335] In Nablus, fourteen of the thirty-five who had been released reportedly responded to a summons to turn themselves back in.[336] Hamas political leader `Abd al-`Aziz al-Rantisi was rearrested on October 18 and released again on December 26, 2000, at the end of Ramadan.[337]

---

[334] Prior to the current uprising, "political" detainees, mostly supporters or suspected supporters of Hamas and Islamic Jihad, were periodically detained in large numbers, usually in the aftermath of attacks against Israeli civilians or military targets and usually without charge or trial. In mid-1997, for instance, between 115 and 300 "political" detainees had been in Palestinian detention for at least one, and as long as three, years. See Human Rights Watch, "Human Rights under the Palestinian Authority," September 1997, p. 11. An estimated seven hundred "political" detainees had been arrested in 1999 and 2000. See Human Rights Watch, "Justice Undermined," November 2001, p. 25. Hamas political leader Mahmud Zahar, speaking to the Palestinian daily al-*Ayyam,* named five released Hamas detainees who he said had spent around five years in prison. See Jersualem Media and Communications Centre (JMCC) Daily Press Summary, October 9, 2000. See also "Terrorists Recently Released by the Palestinian Authority," October 12, 2000 at http://www.mfa.gov.il (accessed October 10, 2002). Several of the individuals listed were released earlier in 2000, according to the IDF at http://www.idf.i./english/idf_in_pictures/2000/october/piguim.stm (accessed September, 2002).

[335] Margot Dudkevitch and Lamia Lahoud, "Mofaz denies PA re-arresting released terrorists," *Jerusalem Post,* October 16, 2000."

[336] Ron Kampeas, "Israelis and Palestinians agree to cease-fire summit," Associated Press, October 14, 2000.

[337] "Released Hamas leader says intifadah only way to unite Palestinians," al-Jazeera interview with `Abd al-`Aziz al-Rantisi, BBC Summary of World Broadcasts, The Middle East, December 29, 2000. A report on the Hamas-affiliated Palestinian Information Centre website on December 28, 2000 said that with al-Rantisi's release, the only Hamas leader still in PA custody in Gaza was Muhammad Deyf, but that Hamas prisoners had not been released from PA prisons in the West Bank. See "Hamas reports fate of jailed leading member Al-Dayf "still unknown," BBC Summary of World Broadcasts, The MiddleEast, December 30, 2000.

The Islamic Jihad organization has cited these releases as a factor contributing to the group's ability to carry out attacks against Israeli targets. The group's military wing, according to an account posted on its website, had suffered "painful blows that led to its breakdown" but with "the support from the masses as well as the release of some strugglers [*mujahidin*] from the PA prisons, the efforts of the movement to rebuild its military strength hastened the establishment of a new military agency, saraya al-quds."[338] In early June 2001, Israel reportedly presented to the PA lists of people it said were responsible for attacks against civilians and military targets, including, according to some reports, as many as one hundred who had been released from PA detention.[339]

As the conflict widened and the toll of Palestinian civilian casualties mounted, reports of arrests by Palestinian security forces declined.[340] In late November 2000, the PA cabinet secretary and Arafat advisor Ahmad `Abd al-Rahman reportedly said that the PA and its Islamist opposition were "fighting in the same trench."[341] In mid-April 2001, the PA confirmed that it had released Muhammad Deyf, imprisoned since 1996 for his role in the Hamas suicide bomb attacks in February of that year, although officials insisted he remained under their control in "a safe place where he cannot be reached by the Israeli authorities."[342] No such pretenses were made when Deyf narrowly escaped death in an Israeli rocket attack targeting him as he traveled by car in Gaza city on September 26, 2002.[343]

Some of the detainees released at the beginning of the uprising, as well as other armed militants and political critics of the PA, were re-detained and re-released periodically during 2001. Some were formally arrested and, beginning in late October 2001, the PA started using administrative detention orders to

---

[338] "From Qassam to Saraya al-Quds," (in Arabic) at http://www.qudsway.com. Translated by Human Rights Watch.

[339] "After the Tel Aviv Suicide-bomb," *Economist* (June 9-15, 2001), p. 46.

[340] On November 27, 2000, the PA announced that it had arrested two Hamas members in connection with a car bombing in Hadera that killed two civilians and wounded sixty. Human Rights Watch does not have information concerning any investigation or prosecution related to this attack.

[341] Holger Jensen, "Chances for Mideast peace dwindle in cycle of violence," *Denver Rocky Mountain News*, November 23, 2000.

[342] "Palestinians confirm Hamas military leader no longer in custody," Agence France-Presse, April 16, 2001.

[343] James Bennet, "Israel says target in Gaza raid was wounded, but escaped," *New York Times*, September 28, 2002. The attack killed two other Hamas members and wounded more than thirty persons, including fifteen children.

detain suspects. Individuals known to be leaders of groups responsible for attacks against civilians nevertheless continued to operate openly in the West Bank and Gaza Strip—in the case of Bethlehem-area al-Aqsa Brigades leader Atef Abayat, even when technically under "house arrest." In Gaza, the PA had issued a warrant in October 2001 for the arrest of `Abdallah al-Shami, but the reputed Islamic Jihad military leader was not taken into custody until June 8, 2002. (See below.)

Those measures taken by the PA to limit armed activities failed to include meaningful efforts to bring perpetrators of suicide attacks on civilians to justice. For example, following the Dolphinarium attack on June 1, 2001, President Arafat issued a statement saying that he would "do all that is needed to achieve an immediate, unconditional, real and effective cease-fire," and that the PA would implement it "by force if necessary."[344] Palestinian security officials at the time said they had boosted their patrols throughout the areas under their jurisdiction. However, they also made clear that they had no plans to arrest any of the large number of militants "wanted" by Israel, some of whom were allegedly responsible for attacks on civilians.[345] Nabil Sha'ath, the PA international cooperation minister, said on June 7, 2001, that two people suspected of involvement in the Dolphinarium attack had been arrested, but he made clear that arrests would be confined to those who had violated the cease-fire that had just been declared. "I don't think we should just be arresting people...unless we have real information, hard information, that some people are preparing something," Sha'ath said.[346] West Bank Preventive Security chief Jibril Rajoub went further by stating, "We will not arrest any Palestinian who participated in the resistance prior to the cease-fire."[347] Even when arrests were

---

[344] "After the Tel Aviv suicide-bomb," *Economist* (June 9-15, 2001), p. 46.

[345] According to the *Economist*, ibid., Israel demanded that the PA "re-arrest the 100 or so Hamas and Islamic Jihad prisoners freed from PA jails" early in the uprising as well as "another 200 Palestinians, including members of Fatah and officers in the PA's own security forces, who Israel says have been responsible for killing Israelis, whether in Israel or the Occupied Territories." Other accounts said the lists included thirty-four Palestinians whom the PA had released from detention at the outset of the uprising and 300 others wanted in connection with "recent violence against military and civilian targets." See "Chronology: 16 May-15 August 2001," *Journal of Palestine Studies* XXXI, no. 1, Autumn 2001, p.160.

[346] "Palestinians will not make wholesale arrests but will hunt suspects: Shaath," Agence France-Presse, June 9, 2001.

[347] "Israel-Palestine divided over agenda for security talks," Agence France-Presse, June 18, 2001.

made, there is little evidence to suggest that individuals responsible for suicide attacks against civilians were ever investigated, charged, or tried.

In late September 2001, the Israeli government reportedly again passed to the PA lists of people it wanted arrested. The PA initiated another round of arrests, although it was unclear if those arrested were named on those lists. The arrests sparked violent opposition. In the Rafah area of southern Gaza, crowds set fire to PA intelligence agency offices. In Bethlehem, al-Aqsa Brigades leader Atef Abayat was detained on October 2, but only after extensive negotiations with Abayat's armed followers; he was held for only a very brief period despite President Arafat's reported order that he be kept in custody.[348]

During a Human Rights Watch field mission to the West Bank in January 2002, local human rights activists said that many of those detained in late 2001 had been arrested for low-level political activities; few held significant roles in armed groups, and fewer still faced formal charges. When the PA did make arrests, it was generally immediately after suicide attacks against civilians, in apparent response to Israeli and international pressure to do so. For the most part, these arrests were of known adherents or supporters of the group claiming responsibility for the attack rather than individuals actually suspected of ordering, planning, or assisting it. One recent exception to this pattern occurred after Islamic Jihad claimed responsibility for a June 5, 2002, bombing of a civilian bus near Megiddo that killed thirteen IDF soldiers and four civilians. On that occasion, PA security forces detained two Islamic Jihad members in Gaza, including `Abdallah al-Shami, the reputed leader of the group's military wing, for whom an arrest warrant had been issued the previous October.

Attempts to arrest perpetrators often encountered considerable resistance from supporters of the militants. Residents of Jenin told Human Rights Watch that when Palestinian Preventive Security in Nablus in November 2001 arrested Mahmud Tawalba, an Islamic Jihad leader from the Jenin refugee camp, demonstrators marched on the PSS headquarters in Jenin, overturning vehicles and threatening to overrun the facility. "The whole camp, even Fatah, came out against this," Abu Antun, a Jenin camp leader, told Human Rights Watch. "Maybe the charges against him were true, but we would do the same for anyone, regardless of affiliation."[349] Tawalba's mother told Human Rights

---

[348] On the 'Abayat arrest, see James Hider, "Mideast truce firms up as Bush backs Palestinian state," Agence France-Presse, October 2, 2001. A Jerusalem-based Western diplomat familiar with the incident told Human Rights Watch that Abayat had been freed by Bethlehem authorities despite Arafat's orders to the contrary.

[349] Human Rights Watch interview, Jenin refugee camp, June 11, 2002. Tawalba was killed in the early days of the IDF invasion of Jenin refugee camp in April 2002. Abu

Watch that on this occasion he had been "ambushed" by the PSS in Nablus and spent three months in jail there. "[CIA head George] Tenet checked his arrest himself," she said proudly. "But when Israel attacked the prison, the jailers left, the prisoners escaped, and Mahmud returned to Jenin."[350]

Haidar Irshaid, the acting governor of Jenin, told Human Rights Watch in June 2002 that the first and last time the PA had arrested armed militants in Jenin was in August 2001, when he led a force of about one hundred security personnel to arrest a group of eight Islamic Jihad activists in Jenin refugee camp. "I knew who we wanted and got them. I visited Arafat in Ramallah and told him about the scene here. 'How much do you need?' he asked. 'How much time?' We did it the next day. Until that time, no such operation was made in all the West Bank."[351] Irshaid did not explain why no other policing efforts had been made prior to this initiative, for which he took credit, but instead blamed Israeli restrictions and the destruction of places of detention for the absence of Palestinian law enforcement initiatives.

The strongest evidence that the PA still retained some law enforcement capacity with regard to attacks against civilians came in December 2001 and early January 2002, when, in contrast to previous periods, the PA undertook sustained efforts to halt suicide bombings and Palestinian attacks in general. In response to a string of Palestinian attacks against settlers, civilians in Israel, and military targets, President Arafat on November 28, 2001, ordered the PSS to arrest members of Hamas, Islamic Jihad, and the al-Aqsa Martyrs' Brigades. On November 29, 2001, following a suicide bombing of a civilian bus in northern Israel, the PA stated, "The Authority reaffirms that it is working in its full capacity to put an end to all sorts of attacks against Israeli civilians."[352] After Hamas suicide bombing attacks on December 1 in Jerusalem, killing ten, and December 2 in Haifa, killing fifteen, Arafat declared a state of emergency, pronounced illegal "any movement, organization, or grouping" that violated the cease-fire he had declared a few days earlier, ordered the confiscation of illegal weapons, and stated that Palestinian security forces had arrested some ninety

---

Antun, formerly affiliated with the PFLP, is considered in Jenin to be an independent figure today.

[350] Human Rights Watch interview, Jenin refugee camp, June 11, 2002.

[351] Human Rights Watch interview, Jenin city, June 10, 2002. Human Rights Watch has been unable to confirm that such an arrest raid took place in Jenin in or around August 2001, but Irshaid's account corresponds to reports of such a raid in early January 2002 (see below).

[352] Carol Rosenberg, "Arab Suicide Bomber Kills Three Israelis, Wounds Other Bus Riders," Knight-Ridder Tribune Business News, November 30, 2001.

people over the previous several days.[353] The efforts of PSS officers to arrest Hamas leader Shaikh Yassin led to clashes with his supporters in which one Hamas supporter was killed. After continuing demonstrations, the PSS pulled back its forces from Yassin's residence.[354]

In a December 3 meeting after Prime Minister Sharon returned from a visit to the United States, the Israeli cabinet issued a statement declaring the PA "an entity that supports terrorism" and authorizing the prime minister to undertake a "much broader scope" of military activity against the Palestinians.[355] Israeli attacks that day included the destruction of PSS barracks near Gaza City, PA and PSS headquarters, and a jail in Jenin. The next day, the IDF shelled the PA headquarters in Ramallah, though not the building where President Arafat was confined.

On December 16, in a televised speech in Arabic marking the end of Ramadan, President Arafat called for "the complete cessation of all military activities, especially suicide attacks, which we have always condemned. We shall not stand for more than one Authority on this land, in this community and this homeland. . . . ."[356] Arafat added that the PA would "punish all planners and executors and hunt down the violators" and announced that he had declared illegal Palestinian militias "that carry out terrorist activities."[357]

The PA continued to close Hamas and Islamic Jihad offices and said on December 18 that it had arrested more than 180 Palestinians since the beginning of the month, but provided no information on investigations or charges related to

---

[353] "Palestinian authority outlaws groups adopting anti-Israeli operations," WAFA [the official news agency of the PA], translation from BBC Monitoring Middle East-Political, December 2, 2001. The Israeli government dismissed the arrests as "a stunt." Peter Hermann, "Israelis avenge attacks, hit Arafat's compound," *Baltimore Sun*, December 4, 2001.

[354] Richard Beeston, "Frail fanatic who strikes fear in Israel," *The Times* (London), December 7, 2001.

[355] Foreign Minister Peres and other Labor party cabinet members reportedly left the meeting to protest this statement, but did not withdraw from the governing coalition. In July 2001, the IDF reportedly submitted to the cabinet a revised "strike plan" entitled, "The Destruction of the Palestinian Authority and Disarmament of all armed forces," to be implemented after the next big suicide attack inside Israel. See "Peace Monitor," *Journal of Palestine Studies* XXXI, no. 1, Autumn 2001, pp. 108-109. See also "Israeli War Plan Revealed," CBSNews, July 12, 2001.

[356] Yassir Arafat speech, at http://www.palestineaffairscouncil.org/president_arafat_addresses_the_p.htm (accessed July 2002).

[357] Ibid.

responsibility for attacks against civilians. The next day, December 19, the PA announced that it had arrested fifteen PSS officers suspected of participating in attacks on Israelis.[358]

As on earlier occasions, these PA moves sparked popular opposition, some of it violent, but this time the PA continued the crackdown. PA efforts to arrest alleged militants, close down charities and similar institutions affiliated with Hamas and Islamic Jihad, and arrest Hamas leader `Abd al-`Aziz al-Rantisi led to three days of clashes in Gaza. On December 21, Palestinian security forces, in circumstances that appeared to violate international standards on the use of firearms, killed six Palestinians and reportedly wounded about ninety.[359] That same day, Hamas announced that it would abide by the cease-fire, and Islamic Jihad reportedly also indicated it would comply.[360] On December 22, Palestinian security forces in Gaza arrested reputed Islamic Jihad military leader Shadi Muhana and a top aide, Mahmud Judeh.[361] Further PA arrests of Islamic Jihad leaders and militants took place in Jenin, Bethlehem, and elsewhere on January 5, 6, and 10, 2002.[362]

Over a four-week period, from December 16, 2001 to January 15, 2002, no suicide or other attacks inside Israel took place. The IDF said that there were

---

[358] On December 30, PA sources said the authorities had tried and sentenced five PSS officers to eighteen-month jail terms and fired two other officers, one of whom was sentenced to a year in prison, for "anti-Israeli activities." One of those dismissed may have been Nasr 'Awais, a prominent al-Aqsa Brigades member in Nablus. See Mohammed Daraghmeh, "Link to the Fatah movement is spiritual, not organizational.... The al-Aqsa Brigades: Palestinian blood to answer Israeli explosives" (in Arabic), Arab Media Internet Network, March 23, 2002 at http://www.amin.org/mohammed.daraghmeh/2002/mar/mar23.html (accessed on September 8 2002).

[359] Steve Weizman, "Palestinians say militants' truce call puts onus for peace on Israel," Associated Press, December 22, 2001.

[360] James Bennet, "New clashes in Gaza; Hamas to limit suicide attacks," *New York Times*, December 22, 2001. The Hamas statement referred to attacks inside Israel, including mortar attacks, but implied that it did not consider itself bound to refrain from attacks against military targets or settlers in the Occupied Territories. The PA reportedly backed down after attempting to arrest Hamas political leader `Abd al-`Aziz al-Rantisi, in the end cutting his phone line and getting his agreement not to conduct media interviews. Lee Hockstader, "Funeral violence averted in Gaza; Many seethe but six Palestinians are buried without incident," *Washington Post*, December 23, 2001.

[361] Ross Dunn, "Arafat to defy ban and walk to Bethlehem," *Sydney Morning Herald*, December 24, 2001.

[362] On the Jenin arrests, see Lamia Lahoud and Margot Dudkevitch, "PA arrests 6 Islamic Jihad militants," *Jerusalem Post*, January 7, 2001; on Bethlehem see Karin Laub, "Mideast truce top goal of US envoy," Associated Press, January 5, 2002.

several attempts to attack settlements and military targets, but reported on December 30 that there had been a 50 percent drop in Palestinian attacks since December 16.[363] Prime Minister Sharon claimed that this was due to Israeli military activities rather than PA efforts.[364]

The cease-fire broke on the Palestinian side on January 9, when two Hamas fighters killed four Israeli soldiers in an ambush in Israel, near the border with Gaza—retaliation, Hamas claimed, for the IDF's treatment of the bodies of three Gaza teenagers killed by a tank shell on December 30, 2001.[365] The next day, the IDF razed fifty-nine homes in the Rafah refugee camp, and the Palestinian factions—except Fatah and the al-Aqsa Martyrs' Brigades—announced they would no longer consider themselves bound by the cease-fire commitment.

On January 14, following the assassination of the Tulkarem leader of the al-Aqsa Martyrs' Brigades, Ra'id Al-Karmi, that group announced that it was also canceling its adherence to the cease-fire. Al-Aqsa Martyrs' Brigades gunmen abducted and shot to death an Israeli settler near Beit Sahur on January 15. On January 17, an al-Aqsa Brigades gunman attacked a bat mitzvah celebration in the Israeli city of Hadera, killing six and wounding several dozen before being shot to death by Israeli police. On January 22, an al-Aqsa Brigades gunman opened fire in west Jerusalem; two of the sixteen Israelis who were wounded later died. The violence on both sides continued to escalate with the first suicide bombing of the new year, a January 25 attack on a Tel Aviv street claimed by Islamic Jihad, which wounded twenty-five, some critically. On January 27, Wafa' Idris carried out the first suicide bombing claimed by the al-Aqsa Brigades, and the first in which a woman was the perpetrator.

Palestinian officials and Fatah leaders blamed the breakdown of the December 2001-January 2002 cease-fire on what they charged were repeated Israeli violations, including several assassinations, an attempted assassination in which two children were killed, and a number of IDF incursions into PA-

---

[363] "Six Palestinians killed, Israel says," *St. Petersburg Times* (Florida), December 31, 2001.

[364] "Sharon tells Norway's foreign minister that Arafat has done nothing," Agence France-Presse, January 2, 2002.

[365] The IDF initially said the three were armed, but subsequently said no weapons were found on them. See "Three Palestinians killed in Gaza were from Popular Resistance Committee," Agence France-Press, December 31, 2001. The IDF returned the bodies of the three on January 3, 2002. Photographs of the three bodies led to charges that their bodies had been mutilated. On January 23, 2002, the IDF announced the results of an investigation, saying that they had been killed by tank shells packed with flechettes, and that one of the bodies had been run over by a tank.

controlled areas, culminating in the assassination of al-Karmi.[366] "[The cease-fire] came out of real efforts by the PA," a top PSS official told Human Rights Watch. "Thirty-two Hamas and Jihad institutions were closed and we controlled the mosques. We asked for seven days [reference to Prime Minister Sharon's insistence on "seven days of absolute quiet"] and we got three weeks. It was Fatah people like Marwan Barghouti who made it happen. The Israeli 'thank you' was to assassinate al-Karmi. You think we can arrest somebody today? This is fantasy."[367]

Some Israelis also saw the al-Karmi assassination as pivotal. Aluf Benn, diplomatic correspondent of the Israeli daily *Ha'aretz*, wrote retrospectively that it "was the war's turning point."[368] Several days after al-Karmi's killing, Dalia Rabin-Pelosoff, then Israel's deputy minister of defense, said, "Every time there appears to be some sort of respite on the ground, something happens, whether by us or by the other side. Recently, in my opinion, we missed an opportunity to make a turning point."[369] Whether or not one accepts this analysis, the cycle of violence that ensued sharply reduced the PA's capacity to confront the perpetrators and sponsors of attacks against civilians.

PA officials have claimed that they had prepared plans to continue the campaign of arrests of December 2001 and early January 2002, but were unable to do so because of repeated large-scale IDF incursions into West Bank cities, refugee camps, and villages, and increased Palestinian popular hostility toward any PA efforts to restrict the activities of the armed militants. This has remained their refrain when asked about the absence of any steps by the PA against the perpetrators of suicide bombings. Muhammad `Abd al-Nabi, a Fatah leader in Dheisheh refugee camp outside Bethlehem, speaking with Human Rights Watch

---

[366] During the cease-fire period, one Israeli soldier was killed on December 25, by infiltrators from Jordan. At least twenty-one Palestinians were killed by Israelis during this period. Most, Israel claimed, were armed or "wanted" militants, but the toll included two children killed when an IDF helicopter-fired missile missed its intended target and hit the car in which they were riding in Hebron on December 17.

[367] Human Rights Watch interview, Jerusalem, June 9, 2002. West Bank PSS head Jibril Rajoub told an Egyptian newspaper at the time that more than forty-five Hamas and Islamic Jihad offices "that have political or media activities" had been closed down, but that "charity institutions that offer health or education services" were not. See "Palestinian Security Chief on Cease-fire Decision, Compliance of Hamas," *Al-Musawwar* (Cairo), December 28, 2001. Excerpts translated by Foreign Broadcast Information Service (FBIS), document number: FBIS-NES-2002-0102.

[368] "In Israel, Too Much to Leave to the Generals," *Washington Post,* August 18, 2002.

[369] Rabin-Pelosof's comments on Israel radio were reported in Peter Hermann, "Israel takes Arab city; Army's incursion in West Bank is its deepest since 1993," *Baltimore Sun,* January 22, 2002.

on June 12, 2002, claimed that five days earlier "all security units were put on alert, and the governor had an arrest list ready—including Fatah." The arrest plans were interrupted by yet another IDF incursion into Bethlehem, he said. Neither he nor other officials in Bethlehem explained the PA's failure to make such efforts prior to the IDF's reoccupation of the area, and `Abd al-Nabi expressed some relief at having the excuse of Israeli interference. "If Sharon had not done that I'd be in a very hard place," he said. "Hamas and [Islamic] Jihad— they should send him a thank-you."[370]

Security officials in Bethlehem told Human Rights Watch that in fact a few arrests were nonetheless continuing—discreetly. Majid Hamad Attari, the head of the Preventive Security Service (PSS) in Bethlehem, told Human Rights Watch on June 13, 2002, that the previous day his forces had arrested an Islamic Jihad activist with explosives, who was being held in detention. When Human Rights Watch asked if this arrest had been reported, Attari replied, "It's not helpful to publicize these arrests." The authorities, he said, needed "to keep a good face before the Palestinian community while doing its duties."[371] Attari's statement reflected the PA's continuing reluctance to signal unequivocally that it firmly opposed attacks against civilians.

Human Rights Watch's discussions with PA and Fatah officials in June 2002 indicated that the PA's failure to move against the perpetrators of attacks against civilians was most acute in the northern part of the West Bank, in contrast with the central region. PA officials and others in Jenin, for instance, indicated that there had been no notable PA law enforcement initiatives in that area since early January 2002. The PA-appointed governor, Zuhair Manasra, had left the district early in 2002, a consequence, Palestinians there said, of the widespread and often violent hostility among supporters of all factions, including Fatah, to PA policies aimed at returning to political negotiations with Israel. Media accounts confirm the view of independent observers that the political authority of the PA was extremely limited in Nablus as well. PA security installations were also destroyed or heavily damaged in Bethlehem, as in the north, but officials in Bethlehem claimed to be taking measures, however limited, to prevent Palestinian attacks against civilians. This picture of a differential PA political and law enforcement capacity is consistent with reports of other analysts.[372] Not coincidentally, Bethlehem was the one locale where the

---

[370] Human Rights Watch interview, Dheisheh refugee camp, June 12, 2002.

[371] Human Rights Watch interview, Bethlehem, June 13, 2002.

[372] Khalil Shikaki, an independent political analyst based in Ramallah, and Graham Usher, the *Economist* correspondent based in Jerusalem, made such observations in conversations with Human Rights Watch in June and July 2002.

PA, in August 2002, publicly resumed some security-related activities under the terms of an agreement negotiated between Israeli Defense Minister Binyamin Eliezer and PA Interior Minister `Abd al-Razaq al-Yahya.

Palestinian Authority Payments to Armed Militants

The available evidence of direct PA financial support for armed activities against Israel consists of some twenty documents made public by the government of Israel. The documents detail multiple requests for financial aid to President Arafat or other Fatah leaders between May 2001 and January 2002. [373] In all, seventeen documents contained requests for financial assistance on behalf of 157 individuals or their families; four contained requests for funding in the name of the al-Aqsa Martyrs' Brigades.

No requests in the name of the al-Aqsa Martyrs' Brigades for financial assistance were approved. Six requests on behalf of individuals, totaling sixty-eight individual payments, were approved or authorized. Twenty-seven of these payments were to families of militants who had been killed or jailed, and forty-one were to individuals, many of whom were characterized as "brothers" or "wanted." The available evidence does not indicate whether such financial assistance was of a one-time nature or routine. Almost all individuals appear to be members or activists within the Fatah movement. During the time period of the payments, in the final months of 2000 and throughout 2001, members of the Fatah-affiliated al-Aqsa Martyrs' Brigades carried out shooting attacks against civilians in the Occupied Territories as well as against military targets, and in late November 2001 the al-Aqsa Martyrs' Brigades claimed responsibility for an indiscriminate shooting attack against civilians in the Israeli city of Hadera.

Fatah officials authorized these six requested payments despite widely available evidence that, in at least the cases of two individuals, the named recipients had participated in attacks on civilians in the Occupied Territories. Fourteen of the forty-one individuals for whom payment was authorized were at the time "wanted" by Israel. Twelve of these individuals, in seeking financial assistance, identified themselves as "wanted." Neither the documents nor the accompanying Israeli commentary indicate whether they were wanted for attacks on civilians or for other alleged offenses. In the cases of Ra'id al-Karmi and Atef Abayat, however, President Arafat and other responsible officials knew or should have known of their widely reported (and in al-Karmi's case, self-

---

[373] The IDF has also publicized payments that appear to have involved the misuse of PA funds, including the use of the PA salaries to fund Fatah branch activities in 1998 and 1999, at a time when Fatah activists openly supported the PA's adherence to the Oslo Accords and security cooperation with Israel.

proclaimed) responsibility for perpetrating shooting attacks that targeted Israeli civilians. In both cases, the government of Israel had previously requested their arrest. Other times, Fatah officials had the capacity to check the background of the individuals named on the list, and thus could have ensured that no assistance would go to people who were responsible for attacks against civilians. At least two lists are extensively annotated, and unnamed functionaries are asked to present other names in order of merit.[374]

The clearest case in which President Arafat authorized payment despite the recipient's widely reported links to attacks on civilians was that of Ra'id al-Karmi, the al-Aqsa Brigades leader in Tulkarem.[375] An undated request from Ramallah-based Fatah leader Hussein al-Sheikh asked Arafat to provide al-Karmi and two others with $2,500 each; Arafat apparently authorized payments of $600 each on September 19, 2001.[376] The IDF had placed al-Karmi on its "most wanted" list in August 2001, accusing him of involvement in "numerous" shooting attacks and responsibility for the deaths of seven civilians and two soldiers. Al-Karmi himself openly boasted of his involvement in the execution-style killing of two Israeli restaurateurs visiting Tulkarem on January 23, 2001—in retaliation, he said, for Israel's assassination several seeks earlier of local Fatah leader Thabet Thabet.[377] The PA had arrested al-Karmi and three others later in January 2001 in connection with the killing of the two restaurateurs, but he fled prison several months later. Al-Karmi had survived a well-publicized Israeli assassination attempt on September 6, 2001, shortly before President Arafat authorized the payment in question, and had spoken openly of his intention to continue attacks against Israelis.[378]

---

[374] Some typical handwritten annotations next to individual names on the memo are "good fighter" and "we know him."

[375] See "Arafat's Documents, Continuation" (in Arabic), IDF at http://www.idf.il/arafat/continuation/english/index1.stm (accessed October 10, 2002).

[376] Government of Israel, "The Involvement of Arafat, PA Senior Officials and Apparatuses in Terrorism against Israel, Corruption and Crime," prepared by a team headed by Minister of Parliamentary Affairs (n.d.), Dani Naveh, p. 20. (Hereafter cited as Naveh.)

[377] Al-Karmi also claimed that the restaurateurs were undercover intelligence agents. Israel claimed at the time that Thabet had been involved in attacks against Israeli targets. Human Rights Watch wrote to the government of Israel on January 29, 2001 requesting evidence for this allegation but did not receive a response. See Human Rights Watch press release and letter, "Israel: End 'Liquidation' of Palestinian Suspects," January 29, 2001.

[378] Greg Myre, "Palestinians Die in Airstrike" Associated Press Online, September 6, 2001.

In another captured document, al-Karmi approached Arafat via Marwan Barghouti, requesting payments to twelve "fighter brethren," not including himself.[379] Despite al-Karmi's own self-proclaimed responsibility for attacks on civilians, Arafat granted a payment of $350 to each individual on al-Karmi's list, again without making any apparent effort to ensure that these fighters were not responsible for attacks on civilians. The payments were made on January 7, 2002, a week before al-Karmi was assassinated. At the time of his assassination, according to media reports, the PA had assured European Union officials that al-Karmi was under arrest.[380] According to one report, he was assassinated "while visiting his wife and daughter during a furlough from the 'protective custody' of a PA jail."[381]

Atef Abayat was a Bethlehem-area al-Aqsa Brigades leader whose arrest Israel had requested as early as November 2000 after he had been involved in a clash with IDF soldiers near al-Khader village. A July 9, 2001, request by Kamal Hmeid, the head of Fatah in Bethlehem, for assistance of $2,000 each to twenty-four local activists, including Abayat, apparently led to Arafat's authorization of $350 to each.[382] In early August 2001, before Arafat authorized the payment, Abayat had allegedly killed at least one Israeli civilian.[383] Hmeid denied to the media that the funds were used to support armed attacks. "The money we receive is used for political and social activities only," he said, without addressing the fact that the document listed Abayat among the recipients.[384] Five weeks after the payment was authorized, Abayat allegedly

---

[379] See "Arafat's Documents,Continuation" Document 2, IDF at http://www.idf.il/arafat/english/index1.htm (accessed September 25, 2002).

[380] Virginia Quirke, "Militants avenge Israeli killing; Fatah group calls off ceasefire after leader's death, fuelling new upsurge in violence," *Guardian* (London), January 15, 2002.

[381] Graham Usher, "Ending the phony cease-fire," *Middle East International*, January 25, 2002, p. 4.

[382] This document was among those seized by Israeli authorities in the takeover of the Orient House in east Jerusalem in August 2001. Human Rights Watch obtained a poor copy of the original, identified as Appendix A, "Palestinian Authority Captured Documents, Main Implications," IDF 688/0010, April 7, 2002.

[383] Abayat was named by "security sources" as responsible for the February 11, 2001 roadside shooting of electrician Tzahi Sasson on the Jerusalem-Gush Etzion Tunnel Road. See Arieh O'Sullivan, Margot Dudkevitch, and Etgar Lefkovits, "Hiker killed in terror ambush; Tanzim fugitive dies in Bethlehem blast; Shots, mortars fired on Gilo," *Jerusalem Post*, October 19, 2001.

[384] Greg Myre, "Israel says seized document shows Arafat paying militant wanted by Israel," Associated Press, March 21, 2002. "Arafat is too clever to use written documents that would link him to attacks," said Boaz Ganor, head of the Israel-based International

killed another civilian. PA security forces attempted to arrest Abayat on October 2 (see above), but allowed him to go free following a confrontation with his armed supporters. Israeli forces assassinated Abayat on October 18, 2001.

Another person on the list of three for whom President Arafat authorized a $600 payment in September 2001 was Ziad Da`as, a member of the al-Aqsa Brigades in Tulkarem and reportedly the successor to al-Karmi as leader of the group there. At the time when the payment was authorized, so far as Human Rights Watch could determine, Da`as had not been publicly linked with attacks against civilians. However, the February 2002 "memo to Tirawi" (see below) named Da`as as the leader of one of three al-Aqsa Brigades "squads" in Tulkarem and attributed to him a leading role in the deadly shooting attack on civilians claimed by the al-Aqsa Brigades in the Israeli city of Hadera on January 17, 2002. Da`as's name also appears among twenty-five activists listed on a memorandum from Marwan Barghouti requesting President Arafat's approval of financial assistance. The document is undated, and there is no indication of whether Arafat approved the request.

Human Rights Watch identified five cases in which Israeli analysts allege that an individual requesting financial assistance had direct involvement in suicide attacks against civilians.[385] The documents do not indicate whether any of these requests were granted. Of those requests that were dated, each was

---

Policy Institute for Counter-Terrorism, commenting on this document. "He knows how to incite people, how to create the atmosphere, but in a way that doesn't directly point to him."

[385] Nasser Yusuf Abu Hamid (Ramallah) was alleged to have participated in the "direction of suicide attacks inside Israel", Tareq Muhammad Daud and Sharif Muhammad Abu Hamid were alleged to have also been involved in planning suicide attacks. Their names occur on a list of Tanzim members signed by Marwan Barghouti November 7, 2000; no request for payment was made. See Document 4 of "Additional Captured Documents Reveal Again the System of Money Transfers to Terrorist Squads, Personally Authorized by Yasser Arafat, with the Deep Involvement of Marwan Barghouti," IDF TR6-498-02, 24 June 2002. Obtained by Human Rights Watch from the Office of the Prime Minister of Israel. Ashraf Yusuf Hamed Bani Jabr and Ibrahim Mahmud `Abdul-Rahman Diriyah were alleged to be involved in attempts to send "suicide terrorists" into Israel. Their names appear in a request for financial aid dated July 19, 2001; the date of their alleged involvement in the attacks is not specified. There is no indication that the request was approved. See Document 7 "Additional Captured Documents Reveal."

[385] See "The Involvement of Arafat, PA Senior Officials and Apparatuses in Terrorism Against Israel, Corruption and Crime," Chapter II, Document 3 at http://www.mfa.gov.il/mfa/go.asp?MFAH0lom0 (accessed September 20, 2002). An undated request for assistance was made on behalf of Firas Sabri Fa'iz, who allegedly participated in the murder of two Israeli restaurateurs in January 2001. There is no indication of approval.

made several months before the first al-Aqsa Brigades suicide attacks against civilians.

In addition to Da'as, al-Karmi, and Abayat, two individuals listed in the various requests for financial assistance are alleged by the Israeli authorities to have participated in attacks against civilians. Of these two requests, Arafat authorized one: a payment of $800 to Bilal Abu `Amsha on April 5, 2001. Israeli authorities allege that Abu `Amsha was responsible for the shooting of a sixty-three-year-old man on May 31, 2001, seven weeks after the payment was authorized.

Requests for financial assistance were typically presented to Marwan Barghouti, in his capacity as secretary-general of Fatah in the West Bank, who then presented them to Arafat. Other senior Fatah figures, such as Hussein al-Sheikh, also forwarded such requests. The size of requested financial assistance differed according to an individual's seniority, but generally ranged from the equivalent of $300 to $800. President Arafat's authorization typically consisted of a handwritten instruction to the "ministry of finance" to make the payment(s) indicated. These recipients were described in the funding requests as, variously, "brothers," "fighting brothers," or simply "pursued by the occupation forces and deserving of aid." Most of the recipients appear to be Fatah-associated, except for two identified by Israeli analysts as PFLP members and one identified by Israeli analysts as an Islamic Jihad member.[386]

Human Rights Watch was unable to ascertain whether such payments and funding practices continued in 2002, after the al-Aqsa Brigades began to carry out suicide bombing attacks against civilians. Several documents from the Fatah branches in the Jenin and Nablus districts, from which many al-Aqsa Brigades attacks against civilians emanated, complained about an absence of funds for armed militants. (See above.)

In the cases of Ra'id al-Karmi and Atef Abayat, President Arafat authorized financial assistance to persons whom he knew or should have known had been involved in attacks against civilians. These payments, while small in amount and few in number, demonstrate Arafat's disturbing indifference to, if not possible support for, Palestinian attacks on civilians.

President Arafat should take immediate steps to ensure that in the future no financial assistance is given to individuals engaged in attacks against civilians, and should enforce and make public a requirement not to attack civilians as a condition of any future payments.

---

[386] See in particular, "International Financial Aid to the Palestinian Authority Redirected to Terrorist Elements," IDF TR2-317-02, May 26, 2002.

Requests for Palestinian Authority Financial Assistance from Armed Groups

According to press reports, President Bush was shown Israeli intelligence reports of a direct payment of $20,000 made or authorized by President Arafat to the al-Aqsa Martyrs' Brigades shortly after two suicide attacks against civilians claimed by the Brigades.[387] Evidence supporting this allegation of payment has not been made public.

Of the body of materials released publicly by the IDF, two documents on al-Aqsa Brigades letterhead were allegedly discovered by the IDF in the main PA compound. The IDF has claimed that the documents:

> Reveal that the Al-Aqsa Brigades is an established organization, which holds official correspondence with Fu'ad Shubaki's office in order for it to finance its planned operations. This money does not go merely to finance propaganda concerning terrorists involved in attacks, but also to control the planning of future attacks.[388]

One undated memo, on letterhead emblazoned in Arabic and English "al-Aqsa Martyres [sic] Troops Palestine," consists of a handwritten costing of salaries, rent, and tools such as lathes and milling machines, totaling some $80,000.[389] The IDF analysis asserts that the items indicate "an ambitious plan... to establish a heavy arms production workshop," including mortars.[390]

The second document is a financial report, typed on similar letterhead and dated September 16, 2001.[391] It reports debts of 38,000 Israeli shekels ($8,800 US dollars), indicating, at a minimum, that the al-Aqsa Brigades considered they had a reporting relationship with the recipient. The breakdown of expenses includes the production of martyrs posters, memorial ceremonies, "electrical parts and various chemical materials" for manufacturing explosives, and

---

[387] Todd S. Purdum and Patrick E. Tyler, "Aides to Bush Say Arafat Financed a Terrorist Group," *New York Times*, June 26, 2002.

[388] IDF Communique, "Yasser Arafat's "Mukata'a" Compound in Ramallah – A Center for Controlling and Supporting Terrorism," April 2, 2002 at http://www.mfa.gov.il/mfa/go.asp?MFAH0lg70, (September 20, 2002). Note that original text spelled al-Aksa Brigades and Fu'ad Shoubaki differently.

[389] "Arafat and the PA's Involvement in Terrorism (According to Captured Documents)," Appendix B, Document 1, IDF 688/0018, April 22, 2002. Human Rights obtained a hard copy from the Office of the Prime Minister, Jerusalem.

[390] Ibid.

[391] Ibid.

ammunition.[392]   The report also requests an immediate transfer of funds to purchase Kalashnikov bullets.

Neither document was signed. There is no indication in the scanned originals of the office(s) or individual(s) to whom the documents were addressed or whether they were ever approved. The IDF has said that the documents were addressed to Fu'ad Shubaki, and seized from the government compound in Ramallah. Shubaki, a close associate of Arafat, held the official title of head of the financial directorate of the General Security Service, but has frequently been characterized in media reports as Arafat's chief financial officer. [393]

If it can be verified that the two documents were addressed to high-ranking PA officials, they would represent the clearest available evidence of some level of financial and hence operational relationship between officials of the PA and the al-Aqsa Martyrs' Brigades. The dates of the documents place them prior to the al-Aqsa Brigades' involvement in suicide bombing attacks against civilians, although at a time when the al-Aqsa Brigades did routinely carry out shooting attacks against civilians as well as military targets in the West Bank and Gaza Strip.

A third document, the aforementioned "memo to Tirawi," indicates that in Tulkarem a funding relationship existed between Fatah and some local al-Aqsa Brigades groups. The memo notes that "the Tanzim secretariat provides...sums of money from the Tanzim and emergency budgets as allocations to the armed brothers." [394] The memo does not indicate how much money is provided, or that there are any restrictions or conditions attached, although it does indicate that the sums were "small," leading to disputes among competing groups of al-Aqsa Brigades militants. Elsewhere the memo states that while most of the militants owned their own rifles, contributions from Tanzim and "financial assistance collected from his excellency the president" helped to defray the cost of three additional rifles. It is not clear from the memo whether President Arafat was aware of the purpose of this collection, or when these funds were "collected."

---

[392] Ibid.

[393] Shubaki, at the time of writing, was one of six Palestinian prisoners detained under international supervision in Jericho as a result of alleged involvement in the Karine-A affair, an attempt to smuggle weapons banned under the Oslo Accords into PA areas. For a   summary   of   Israeli   allegations   against   Shubaki,   see http://www.idf.il/project1/english/index.stm (accessed October 11, 2002).

[394] Several partial renditions of this document have been made public by the Israeli government. A complete but poor translation of the Arabic original is available from the Israeli   Ministry   of   Foreign   Affairs   at   http://www.israel-mfa.gov.il/mfa/go.asp?MFAH0llo0. Translated by Human Rights Watch.

In the view of Human Rights Watch, the PA had an obligation to check where funds it controlled were going and how they were being spent. Many PA officials were also leading members of Fatah. In that capacity, they also had a responsibility to check the backgrounds of individuals and groups to ensure that neither PA nor Fatah funding went to individuals or groups that had been involved in attacks against civilians. Regrettably, President Arafat and other senior Fatah officials did provide financial assistance to people involved in planning and carrying out armed attacks that included attacks on civilians (other than suicide bombings). In doing so, these officials seriously abrogated their responsibility as the governing authority to prevent such attacks. However, the publicly available evidence is not conclusive as to whether President Arafat or the PA provided financial support to the perpetrators of attacks against civilians with the intent of supporting such attacks.

Participation of PA Security Officials in Suicide Bombings or Other Attacks on Civilians

Based on its own investigation as well as media accounts and publicly available, captured PA documents, Human Rights Watch identified instances in which individuals employed in one or another Palestinian security force were involved in shooting or suicide bomb attacks targeting civilians. Human Rights Watch also found that individual members of the PA security forces have had ongoing associations with armed groups that have carried out suicide bombing attacks on civilians. On at least two occasions, individual members of PA intelligence services assisted perpetrators in carrying out such attacks.[395]

The PA should have made credible efforts to reprimand, discipline, or, where appropriate, bring to justice members of its own security services who, in apparent disregard for declared PA policies, participated in or lent support to those responsible for attacks against civilians. Insofar as Human Rights Watch could determine, it did not do so.

The IDF has made its most specific allegations about PA security forces' involvement in attacks against civilians with regard to the General Intelligence Services (GIS), a force of about one thousand. The West Bank head of the GIS is Tawfiq Tirawi. An IDF spokesperson's statement of July 2, 2002, claimed that "in the past two years the [GIS] apparatus has been involved in hundreds of shooting and bombing attacks against Israeli civilian and military targets" and that "commanders of the Palestinian General Intelligence, including the head of

---

[395] According to statistics compiled by B'Tselem, PA security forces gunfire was responsible for a total of ten Israeli civilian deaths inside Israel and none in the West Bank or Gaza.

the organization, directed terror cells in various locations in the West Bank."[396] During the IDF siege of President Arafat's headquarters in late September 2002, Israel named Tirawi as among those people in Arafat's remaining building who were "wanted" for alleged "terrorist" activity.

The charges against Tirawi, which he has denied, appear to be based primarily on the results of IDF or Shin Bet interrogations of captured Palestinians. In commentary on documents the IDF says it captured from PA offices in April 2002, Israeli analysts wrote that "wanted terrorist activists who were detained in Operation Defensive Wall reported in their interrogation of the direct involvement of Tirawi and his men in recruiting terrorists, their preparation, and the supply of ammunition for their operations."[397]

The most incriminating document made public by the Israeli authorities— the "memo to Tirawi"—suggests that Tirawi may have viewed attacks on civilians positively. Hamdi Darduk, the head of the GIS in Tulkarem, describes to Tawfiq Tirawi the competitive dynamics among the local armed militants, numbering fifteen to twenty in all. Referring to one group of militants who are willing to operate "on bypass roads and even in the depth of Israel," Darduk notes that they have been responsible for such "qualitative and successful activities," as the shooting attack on a bat mitzvah celebration in Hadera on January 17, 2002. Darduk said that these "men are very close to us and [we are] in constant coordination and contact with them."

The memo expresses frustration that there is "no clear address" for the al-Aqsa Brigades in Tulkarem, and characterizes the attitude of al-Aqsa Brigades militants towards the Tulkarem security services as "defiant and quarrelsome." Darduk complains that the armed factions "stand united vis-à-vis any problem arising with the security services" but "revert to their [divided] state" once the immediate tension with the authorities is resolved. He recommends that the "the outstanding individuals" be selected "to train them for the future" and names

---

[396] The statement claimed that Tirawi "personally directed" Mustafa Mardi, a PFLP activist captured on June 11, to carry out shooting attacks. Mardi allegedly confessed that he had participated in several attacks, including the kidnapping and murder of a teenager from the Pisgat Zeev settlement. Mardi also allegedly confessed that Tirawi had given him a rifle and assigned him to a cell of armed activists in the Ramallah area. Tirawi responded that "the entire Shin Bet statement is a lie from A to Z," and that the GIS had itself arrested Mardi in the past. See Amos Harel, "Israel is targeting Tirawi as a wanted man," *Ha'aretz*, July 3, 2002.

[397] "Operation Defensive Wall datainees demonstrate unequivocally the involvement of the PA General Intelligence in direct and indirect assistance to terrorist activities," IDF Captured Document (undated), circa April 2002, http://www.idf.il/Involvment/english/main_index.stm (accessed May 30, 2002)."

Ziad Da'as and Bilal Abu 'Amsha (see above) among those to be selected. [398] The memo recommends "weeding out some of the outsiders" to "discard their financial burden and the problems they cause," and providing financial and other support to the most desirable individuals

There is no record of any response by Tirawi to this memorandum, or indication that he read it, but the contents show that in Tulkarem the GIS was well aware of who was who among the armed militants affiliated with Fatah and was keen to work with them despite the involvement of some in attacks on civilians. The memo suggests that the GIS was at that time not playing a leading or controlling role in attacks by the al-Aqsa Brigades; rather, tone and content reflect an attempt to assert influence in a situation over which they had lost control. There is no indication, however, that preventing Palestinian attacks against Israeli civilians is among the goals of the GIS in Tulkarem. On the contrary, the writer, addressing the senior GIS officer for the West Bank expressly condoned attacks on civilians, recommended financial support for the perpetrators, and displayed no hesitation about conveying that approval to his superiors.

If this memo accurately reflects GIS policy, it would indicate that at least one PA security service intentionally assisted or sought to assist armed activity by al-Aqsa Brigades militants that included attacks against civilians. [399]

Majid Hamad Attari, the head of Preventive Security in Bethlehem, told Human Rights Watch that his agency's clear instructions since the beginning of the current uprising were to stop attacks against Israelis—"all attacks, not just inside Israel, and not just against civilians." The only times when this broke down, he said, was when the IDF launched attacks directly against Palestinian forces. "The orders even then were, 'Get out of the way, do not resist,'" Attari said, but he indicated that some officers did on those occasions return fire.

---

[398] Ziad Da'as was killed by Israeli forces in Tulkarem on August 8, 2002. There are varying accounts as to whether he was assassinated or executed, as Palestinian witnesses told local journalists, or whether he had been shot while trying to escape. See *Duluth News-Tribune*, August 8, 2002 (accessed October 8, 2002).

[399] The memo does not bear any indication of circulation or approval. Of some seventy different documents made public by Israel that Human Rights Watch has examined, including documents provided by Israeli officials in response to Human Rights Watch's request for the strongest available evidence of systematic PA involvement in, or support for, suicide bombings against civilians, it is the only one that indicates such involvement by the PA authorities.

Human Rights Watch has documented instances in which PSS employees participated in exchanges of fire with IDF forces.[400]

Several people interviewed by Human Rights Watch indicated that the PA policy against the participation of security forces in clashes had led many to quit the forces. One person identified by the IDF as a PSS employee wanted for al-Aqsa Brigades activities is `Ata Abu Rumaila. In an interview with Human Rights Watch in Jenin refugee camp, Rumaila introduced himself as a senior Fatah member there. He acknowledged that he had been in the *mukhabarat* (intelligence services), but said he had resigned and no longer served in any official capacity.[401] "There were a large number of defections," said `Awni al-Mashni, a Fatah leader in Dheisheh refugee camp. Al-Mashni distinguished between those who quit the forces to join "the resistance" and those who had responded when under Israeli attack but otherwise did not take part in attacks against Israelis and who remained on the force.[402]

At least two members of the al-Aqsa Martyrs' Brigades organized or carried out suicide attacks against Israeli civilians while reportedly serving in low-level positions in the PA. Said Ramadan, an employee of the PA naval police, carried out an indiscriminate shooting attack in Jerusalem on January 22, 2002. Ibrahim Hassouna, a Nablus-based employee of the naval police, carried out a shooting attack against civilians at the Sea Market restaurant in Tel Aviv on March 5, 2002.[403] The cases of Ramadan and Hassouna indicate that the al-Aqsa Brigades recruited from the ranks of low-level PA security employees.[404]

---

[400] For example, during an IDF arrest raid in Artas, near Bethlehem, on January 29, 2002.

[401] Human Rights Watch interview, Jenin refugee camp, June 11, 2002. The term *mukhabarat* is frequently used to refer generically to state security agencies as well as to formally designated intelligence agencies. Abu Rumaila noted that several attacks had been launched from Jenin against the nearby Israeli town of Afula in response, he said, to Israeli attacks. The IDF website cites, but does not provide, a captured document about a suicide bomb attack in Afula "in which PA intelligence apparatus activists from Jenin were involved together with the PIJ [Islamic Jihad]."

[402] Human Rights Watch interview, Dheisheh refugee camp, June 13, 2002. An example of those who have left the employ of the PA security services to work with the armed activists is Jamal Abu Samhandanah, a former police major who is now a leader in the Popular Resistance Committee in Gaza. See the *Observer* (London), February 23, 2002.

[403] Lee Hockstader and Daniel Williams, "Mideast fighting intensifies; Both sides vow more," *Washington Post*, March 6, 2002.

[404] One al-Aqsa Brigades statement at the time the IDF launched Operation Defensive Shield "call[ed] on all members of the Palestinian security services to join the ranks of the Brigades." The statement also referred to the Brigades as being "under the leadership

Israel has stated that on April 16, 2002, it captured Muhammad Araj, a member of the GIS, in the Qalandiyya refugee camp outside Ramallah with two belts for carrying explosive devices and two "suicide letters."

Based on documents made public by the IDF, it appears that Arafat approved the recruitment of armed militants for the Palestinian security services in 2001. One example is a list requesting the employment of fifteen individuals sent to Arafat in mid-May 2001 (and again in early August) from Fatah leaders in Hebron. At least two of the individuals named in this document were wanted by Israel for earlier attacks against civilians.[405] One of these, Zaki Hamid al-Zaru, is alleged to have been the sniper who killed a baby girl and wounded her father in a shooting attack against Israeli settlers in Hebron on March 26, 2001.[406] The second, Marwan Zallum, authored the request in his capacity as head of the Fatah district branch in Hebron. Arafat transferred the August version of the memo to various security force commanders "for action." Five months after the May request, Zallum was reportedly placed on a list of Israel's "most wanted" armed Palestinians. He was allegedly involved in the April 12, 2002, suicide attack on the Mahane Yehuda Market, and was assassinated on April 22, 2002.[407] An IDF communiqué on that day listed numerous shootings and other attacks against military targets and civilians, including the Hebron sniper attack of March 26, 2001, which it said were carried out "under [Zallum's] direct orders."[408]

However, the available evidence does not establish that PA recruitment of Fatah activists to the ranks of the PA security forces was done with the intent of supporting or endorsing attacks against civilians. The IDF, in its own analysis of PA recruitment practices, notes that such recruitment appeared to be an effort by PA officials "to integrate Fatah and Fatah/Tanzim activists into the PA's security apparatuses.... The 'deal' offered to them was monthly salary...in

---

of Marwan Barghuti." See "Al-Aqsa Brigades call for unity, name Barghuti as leader for first time," Agence France-Presse, April 1, 2002.

[405]   See   "Document   1"   and   "Document   2" http://www.idf.il/english/announcements/2002/april/Fatah_Activists/3.stm   (accessed October 10, 2002).

[406] For an account of this incident see Human Rights Watch, *Center of the Storm,* pp. 63-65.

[407] Ibid.

[408] See "IDF kills head of military wing Tanzim in the Hebron area," April 22, 2002 at http://www.israel-mfa.gov.il/mfa/go.asp?MFAH0llk0 (accessed October 10, 2002). This summarizes IDF allegations against Zallum.

exchange for the activists operating in accordance with PA policies."[409] The problem, the analysts continue, is that these activists continued to receive PA salaries "even when they refused to participate in activities in the framework of the security forces" and "even while they are included on Israel's list of most wanted terrorists which was transferred to the PA...."[410]

The most prominent example, cited by the IDF analysts, is that of Nasr `Awais, a Nablus-based leader of the al-Aqsa Brigades in the northern West Bank. Israeli forces captured `Awais in April 2002.[411] Israel has accused him of responsibility for sponsoring suicide attacks in Jerusalem, Tel Aviv, and Umm al-Fahm beginning in January 2002. Palestinian sources in Nablus confirmed to Human Rights Watch that `Awais played a leading role in al-Aqsa Brigades operations there, including attacks inside Israel originating in the northern West Bank.[412] According to the IDF, `Awais remained on the payroll of the GIS despite "in recent months" his involvement in planning and carrying out attacks against Israeli civilians.[413] However, some press reports in March 2002 referred to `Awais as a "former" officer.[414] By one account, `Awais was among several PA security employees sacked by Arafat in December 2001.[415] Further investigation is needed to resolve these conflicting allegations.

---

[409] See "The PA employs in its Ranks Fatah Activists Involved in Terrorism and Suicide Attacks" at http://www.idf.il./english/announcements/2002/april/Fatah_Activists/1.stm (accessed October 11, 2002).

[410] Israel considers all political violence directed against Israelis to constitute terrorism, without regard to the civilian or military nature of those targeted.

[411] Devorah Chen, the prosecutor in the trial of Fatah leader Marwan Barghouti, has said that the Israeli government's case would be based on, among other things, testimony of `Awais and other captured militants. See "Palestinian leader indicted on terror charges," Associated Press, August 14, 2002.

[412] Human Rights Watch interviews, names withheld on request, June 2002.

[413] "The Palestinian Authority Employs in its Ranks Fatah Activists Involved in Terrorism and Suicide Attacks" at http://www.idf.il./english/announcements/2002/april/Fatah_Activists/1.stm (accessed October 11, 2002).

[414] Mohammed Daraghmeh, "Palestinian Group: Attacks Won't Stop," Associated Press, March 22, 2002.

[415] See Mohammed Daraghmeh, "Link to the Fatah movement is spiritual, not organizational.... The al-Aqsa Brigades: Palestinian blood to answer Israeli explosives" (in Arabic). Arab Media Internet Network, March 23, 2002 at http://www.amin.org/mohammed.daraghmeh/2002/mar/mar23.html (accessed on September, 8 2002).

Israel has accused Jamal Tirawi, head of GIS in Nablus, and Jihad Masimi, head of criminal investigations for the Nablus police, of having helped to direct suicide bomb operations. [416] Maher Fares, the head of Military Intelligence (MIS) in Nablus, is accused by Israel of operating a cell that placed explosives on a Tel Aviv bus on December 28, 2000, wounding nine. [417] Evidence for the allegations against these three individuals, however, has not been made public. Colonel Abu Hamdan, of MIS in Nablus, is named in captured Palestinian intelligence documents as the leader of the Battalions of the Return, a small, armed group of uncertain provenance. [418]

Security Officials' Protection of Individuals "Wanted" by Israel

Human Rights Watch researchers have documented instances in which PA intelligence officials warned Palestinians that they were "wanted" by Israeli authorities for armed activities. In one case, members the family of R., a reputed member of the al-Aqsa Martyrs' Brigades and planner of suicide attacks against civilians, told Human Rights Watch that he had several times been warned by former colleagues in the General Intelligence Service (GIS) of impending Israeli attempts to capture or assassinate him. [419] Whether such warnings were the result of personal loyalties or official policy was not clear.

Documents made public by Israel also indicate instances in which local security or intelligence officials issued warnings to Palestinians who were "wanted" by Israel, although for the most part there is no indication that this "wanted" status was a result of allegations of involvement in suicide bombings or other attacks on civilians. For example, one letter dated May 21, 2001, from the GIS in Tulkarem to the director of the GIS Ramallah Governorate office, refers to an attached list (not made public) of names of 232 people wanted by Israel. [420] At the bottom of the letter is a handwritten annotation, "Please inform the brothers whose names are mentioned above to stay alert and pay attention.

---

[416] "Nablus, the Infrastructure Center for Palestinian Terrorism," IDF Document, Appendix G, http://www.idf.il/arafat/schem/english/main_index.stm, April 2002 (accessed September 30, 2002). Tirawi and Masimi are both listed as being "alive" and "operational" as of April 2002. Jamal Tirawi, according to the IDF, is a cousin of West Bank GIS chief Tawfiq Tirawi.

[417] Ibid.

[418] Some reports link the Battalions of the Return with dissident Fatah leaders based in Lebanon, while others suggest that it may be an offshoot of Islamic Jihad.

[419] Human Rights Watch interviews, February 4, 2002, Salfit.

[420] "Arafat and the PA's Involvement in Terrorism According to Captured Documents," Appendix B, Document 3, IDF, April 22, 2002.

Also, do a full security check on all those names and let us know."[421] There are no indications as to why those listed were wanted by the Israelis: two were annotated as being affiliated with different PA security services.

Some documents made public by Israel suggest that payoffs by groups to individual security officers, rather than institutional policy, may have been a significant factor in helping members of armed groups evade capture. A memo to West Bank GIS head Tawfiq Tirawi from a person in Jenin whose position and affiliation are not made clear, cites an intelligence source as reporting that "the Hamas and [Islamic] Jihad movements have penetrated the security apparatuses in Jenin, by means of payoffs." The report identifies Jamal Sweitat, deputy head of PSS in Jenin, as one of those people, asserts that he is "working for the [Islamic] Jihad from among General Intelligence and Preventive Security personnel," and says that Sweitat, among other things, "often contacts" Islamic Jihad activists and "notifies [them] of planned arrests against them and who the wanted persons are."[422] Six other intelligence employees are also reported to have received payoffs: three from the GIS, and two from the PSS.[423] Israeli authorities have alleged similar practices in Bethlehem, saying that Islamic Jihad and Hamas made payments of between $1,500 and $3,000 to GIS and PSS officers to ensure that the recipients warned them of any imminent arrest attempts.[424] The IDF has not released evidence for this allegation.

Conclusion

High-ranking PA officials, including President Arafat, failed in their duty to administer justice and enforce the rule of law in compliance with international standards. Through their repeated failure to arrest or prosecute individuals alleged to have planned or carried out suicide attacks against civilians, they contributed a climate of impunity—and failed to prevent the bloody

---

[421] Ibid. Translated by Human Rights Watch.

[422] The Cooperation Between Fatah and the PA Security Apparatuses with PIJ and Hamas in the Jenin Area. IDF document no. 688/0011, TR3-268-02, April 9, 2002. Hard copy obtained by Human Rights from the office of the Prime Minister of Israel. Also see "The PA and the Fatah Security Apparatuses in the Jenin area closely cooperate with Islamic Jihad and Hamas" at http://www.idf.il/jenin/site/english/main_index.stm.

[423] Nayif Sweitat, Jamal's brother and himself a Fatah leader in Jenin, told Human Rights Watch that the document's allegation was "not true" and "part of a *mukhabarat* [GIS] effort to discredit Preventive Security." Human Rights Watch interview, Jenin city, June 11, 2002.

[424] "The Involvement of Arafat, PA Senior Officials and Apparatuses in Terrorism Against Israel, Corruption and Crime (The Naveh File)", p. 32 at http://www.mfa.gov.il/mfa/go.asp?MFAH0lom0.

consequences. Their payments to, and recruitment of, individuals responsible for attacks against civilians likewise demonstrate, at least, a serious failure to meet their political responsibilities as the governing authorities, if not a willingness to support them. However, there is no publicly available evidence that Arafat or other senior PA officials ordered, planned, or carried out such attacks.

Was this failure of President Arafat and the PA so egregious as to establish criminal liability for the actions of armed groups under the doctrine of command responsibility? In relation to Hamas, Islamic Jihad, and the PFLP, there is no suggestion of the supervisor-subordinate relationship that is required to apply the doctrine. The PA could and should have exerted greater political pressure to bring these groups to halt suicide and other attacks on civilians, but that does not reflect the requisite control over their activities. In the case of the al-Aqsa Martyrs' Brigades, any supervisory link appears to have been weak at best. Nor does the PA's capacity to prosecute perpetrators, which it possessed for much of the uprising but did not apply, meet on its own the requirement of "effective control"—the ability to issue instructions, enforce obedience, and punish disobedience—that is necessary for the doctrine of command responsibility to apply. For example, even a government such as Colombia's, with a far more substantial law enforcement capacity, has not been found to have command responsibility for atrocities committed by paramilitary forces simply by virtue of the government's failure to prosecute them.[425] But this is no excuse for inaction: the PA has a clear duty to act, in concert with regional leaders and the international community, to prevent suicide bombing attacks against Israeli civilians, ending the war crimes and crimes against humanity committed by Palestinian armed groups.

---

[425] Human Rights Watch, *The Sixth Division: Military-Paramilitary Ties and U.S. Policy in Colombia* (Human Rights Watch, New York, September 2001).

APPENDIX ONE: CHRONOLOGY OF ATTACKS

Chronology of suicide bombing attacks on civilians and military targets from September 30, 2000 to August 31, 2002.

Dates <u>underlined</u> indicate incidents in which the targets were civilian, indiscriminate, or had a clearly disproportionate effect on civilians. [426] The perpetrators are not included in the casualty count.

October 26, 2000
One IDF soldier was wounded when a suicide bomber from Gaza attacked an IDF post in Shuyaja, Gaza City. Islamic Jihad claimed responsibility.

<u>January 1, 2001</u>
At least twenty people were wounded by a suicide bombing in a bus station in Netanya. Hamas claimed responsibility.

<u>March 4, 2001</u>
Three people were killed and at least sixty wounded when a suicide bomber attacked a shopping mall in Netanya. Hamas claimed responsibility. The bomber was a twenty-two-year-old refugee, Ahmad Ayam, from Tulkarem.

<u>March 27, 2001</u>
At least twenty-eight people were wounded when a bomber detonated explosives in his car adjacent to a bus in East Jerusalem. Hamas claimed responsibility.

<u>March 28, 2001</u>
Two teenagers were killed and four other people wounded when a suicide bomber blew himself up at a gas station one hundred meters from an IDF roadblock at Neve Yamin, near the entrance to Qalqiliya. Hamas claimed responsibility.

April 29, 2001
Only the perpetrator was killed when an attacker drove a car into a school bus in Shavei Shomron settlement, near Nablus. Hamas claimed responsibility.

---

[426] This list was compiled on the basis of press reports and information from the Israeli Ministry of Foreign Affairs.

May 18, 2001
Five were killed and more than one hundred injured when a suicide bomber detonated himself in a Netanya shopping mall. Hamas claimed responsibility.

May 25, 2001
At least forty-five people were wounded when two suicide bombers drove an explosive laden truck into a bus in Hadera. Islamic Jihad claimed responsibility.

June 1, 2001
Twenty one people were killed and at least 120 injured by a suicide bomb attack on the Dolphinarium discotheque in Tel Aviv. Although at first Islamic Jihad claimed the attack, later Hamas said it was responsible.

June 22, 2001
The driver of a jeep apparently stuck in the sand near Dugit, in the Gaza Strip, detonated explosives killing two IDF soldiers who had come to assist. Hamas claimed responsibility for the attack.

July 9, 2001
A truck laden with explosives drove into the Kissufim border crossing in Gaza. Only the perpetrator was killed. Hamas claimed responsibility.

July 16, 2001
A suicide bomber attacked a bus stop in Binyamina, killing two and wounding at least eleven. Although the victims who died were IDF soldiers, some of the wounded were civilians. Islamic Jihad claimed responsibility.

August 9, 2001
Fifteen people were killed and at least 130 injured when a suicide bomber attacked the Sbarro pizzeria on the Jaffa Road in downtown Jerusalem. Islamic Jihad and Hamas issued competing claims of responsibility.

August 12, 2001
Fifteen people were wounded when a twenty-eight-year-old suicide bomber detonated a bomb on the outside patio of a restaurant in Kiryat Motzkin, in Haifa. Islamic Jihad claimed responsibility.

September 4, 2001
At least thirteen people were injured when a suicide bomber disguised himself
by wearing a skullcap and other observant attire and detonated himself in the
ultra-Orthodox area of Me'ah Shearim, in West Jerusalem. Hamas claimed
responsibility.

September 9, 2001
Three people were killed and at least ninety wounded when an Israeli Arab
committed a suicide bombing attack on a group of soldiers and civilians
disembarking a train in the Nahariya station. Hamas claimed responsibility.

October 7, 2001
The driver of a car was killed when a seventeen-year-old suicide bomber blew
himself up near it at the entrance to a kibbutz in the Beit Shean valley, not far
from Jenin. Islamic Jihad claimed responsibility.

October 17, 2001
Two soldiers were wounded by an attack in Gaza. The PFLP claimed
responsibility.

November 8, 2001
Two soldiers were wounded when a suicide bomber blew himself up during a
raid on Baka al-Sharqia, in the West Bank. Hamas claimed responsibility.

November 26, 2001
Two soldiers were wounded by an attack at Erez checkpoint in Gaza. Hamas
claimed responsibility.

November 29, 2001
Three people were killed and at least six injured from a suicide bombing on a
Nazareth-Tel Aviv bus at Pardes Hanna. Islamic Jihad claimed responsibility.

December 1, 2001
Eleven people were killed and more than 130 injured after two suicide bombers
set off sequential explosions followed by a car bomb in a pedestrian mall on Ben
Yehuda street in West Jerusalem. Hamas claimed responsibility.

December 2, 2001
Fifteen people were killed and at least forty wounded by a suicide bomber on a
Haifa city bus. Hamas claimed responsibility.

December 5, 2001
At least two people were wounded by a suicide bomber in a hotel near the old city's Jaffa Gate; the perpetrator, Daoud `Ali Ahmad Abu Suway, was a forty-four year old father of eight children from Artas, near Bethlehem. Islamic Jihad claimed responsibility.

December 9, 2001
At least thirty people were wounded in a suicide bombing attack on a hitch hiking post in Haifa. The suicide bomber, who was not killed by the attack, was killed moments later in disputed circumstances, allegedly as he attempted to detonate more explosives and was shot by the police. Although no group claimed responsibility, the bomber had left a note that the attack was in reprisal for an assassination of a Hamas operative.

December 12, 2001
At least three people were slightly injured when two suicide bombers jumped on a car leaving a Gaza settlement.

January 25, 2002
Twenty five people were wounded by an eighteen-year-old suicide bomber in a Tel Aviv pedestrian mall. Islamic Jihad claimed responsibility for the attack.

January 27, 2002
One person was killed and more than 111 wounded when a suicide bomber blew herself up in downtown Jerusalem. Wafa Idris, the perpetrator, was the first female suicide bomber. The al-Aqsa Martyrs' Brigades claimed responsibility.

February 16, 2002
Three were killed and more than thirty wounded when a eighteen year old suicide bomber attacked a pizzeria in a shopping center in the Karnei Shomron settlement. The perpetrator had died his spiky hair blond, reportedly to be able to blend in. The PFLP claimed responsibility.

February 18, 2002
A policeman was killed when a suicide bomber he had stopped on the road between Maale Adumim settlement and Jerusalem, in the West Bank, detonated his explosives. The al-Aqsa Martyrs' Brigades claimed responsibility.

February 27, 2002
At least three people were wounded by a suicide bomber, Dareen Abu Eishi, who detonated explosives when asked for identity papers at the West Bank Maccabim checkpoint on the Modi'in-Jerusalem road. The al-Aqsa Martyrs' Brigades claimed responsibility.

March 2, 2002
Eleven people, including five children, were killed and at least fifty wounded when a suicide bomber detonated in the ultra-Orthodox neighborhood of Me'ah Shearim in Jerusalem. The attack took place as a bar mitzvah was ending. The suicide bomber was a seventeen-year-old refugee from Bethlehem. The al-Aqsa Martyrs' Brigades claimed responsibility.

March 5, 2002
One person was killed and at least eleven wounded in a suicide bombing attack on Afula bus station. Islamic Jihad claimed responsibility.

March 7, 2002
Fifteen people were wounded in a suicide bombing attack on a hotel on the outskirts of Ariel settlement. The PFLP claimed responsibility.

March 9, 2002
Eleven people were killed and more than fifty injured when a twenty-year-old suicide bomber attacked the crowded Café Moment in Jerusalem. Hamas claimed responsibility.

March 17, 2002
Twenty-five people were wounded when a suicide bomber hurled himself at a bus in East Jerusalem. Islamic Jihad claimed responsibility.

March 20, 2002
Seven were killed and at least twenty-seven wounded by a suicide bomb attack on a bus in Umm al Fahm in Galilee, near Afula. Four of the dead were IDF soldiers, fifteen of the wounded were civilians. Islamic Jihad claimed responsibility.

March 21, 2002
Three were killed and more than sixty injured in an attack on a Jerusalem shopping street. The al-Aqsa Martyrs' Brigades claimed responsibility.

March 22, 2002
One soldier was wounded in a suicide bombing attack on an IDF checkpoint at Salem when he stopped the taxi the bomber used. The al-Aqsa Martyrs' Brigades claimed responsibility.

March 27, 2002
Twenty-nine people were killed and more than one hundred injured by a suicide bomb attack in the Park Hotel in Netanya during a Passover Seder dinner. Hamas claimed responsibility.

March 29, 2002
Two people were killed and at least twenty wounded in an attack at a supermarket in the Kiryat Hayovel district of Jerusalem. The perpetrator was an eighteen-year-old woman. The al-Aqsa Martyrs' Brigades claimed responsibility.

March 30, 2002
One person was killed and at least twenty injured in a suicide bomb attack on a restaurant on Allenby street in Tel Aviv. The al-Aqsa Martyrs' Brigades claimed responsibility.

March 31, 2002
Fifteen people were killed and more than forty-four injured when a suicide bomber struck the Israeli-Arab owned Matza restaurant in Haifa. Hamas claimed responsibility.

March 31, 2002
Four people were wounded in an attack near a volunteer medical station in the Efrat settlement near Bethlehem. The suicide bomber was seventeen years old. The al-Aqsa Martyrs' Brigades claimed responsibility.

April 1, 2002
A police officer died when a suicide bomber detonated himself when stopped at a checkpoint separating East and West Jerusalem. The al-Aqsa Martyrs' Brigades claimed responsibility.

April 10, 2002
Eight people were killed and twenty-two people wounded in an attack near Ha'amaqim junction on a Haifa city bus crowded with commuters. Six of those killed were soldiers. Hamas claimed responsibility.

April 12, 2002
Six people were killed and more than fifty injured in an explosion at a bus stop near the entrance of Mahane Yehuda market in Jerusalem.

May 7, 2002
Fifteen people were killed and at least fifty wounded in an attack on a pool hall in Rishon Letzion. According to Israeli government sources, Hamas claimed responsibility for the attack.

May 19, 2002
Three people were killed and more than thirty wounded by a suicide bomber dressed as an IDF soldier in the Netanya open air market. The bomber was eighteen years old. Both Hamas and PFLP issued claims of responsibility for the attack.

May 20, 2002
A suicide bomber killed only himself when stopped for questioning as he tried to board a bus at Taanakhim junction; the bus was headed for Afula.

May 22, 2002
Two people were killed and at least twenty-four wounded in a suicide bomb attack in Rishon Letzion; the bomber was sixteen years old. A second bomber, who changed her mind before the act, was later arrested. The al-Aqsa Martyrs' Brigades claimed responsibility for the attack.

May 27, 2002
Two people, a baby and her grandmother, were killed and at least thirty-seven were wounded in an attack on the Bravissimo café in Petah Tikva. The bomber, a cousin of an al-Aqsa Brigades operative assassinated several days earlier, was eighteen years old. The al-Aqsa Martyrs' Brigades claimed responsibility for the attack.

June 5, 2002
Seventeen people were killed and at least thirty-eight injured in a suicide attack at Megiddo Junction on a bus headed for Tiberias. Thirteen victims were IDF soldiers. Islamic Jihad claimed responsibility for the attack.

June 11, 2002
One person was killed and fifteen wounded in an attack on a restaurant in Herzliyya. The al-Aqsa Martyrs' Brigades claimed responsibility for the attack.

June 17, 2002
A suicide bomber killed only himself in Kfar Salem, near where Israeli authorities had commenced construction of a security fence, when border police approached him.

June 18, 2002
Nineteen people were killed and seventy-four wounded by a bus traveling to Jerusalem from the nearby Gilo settlement. Hamas claimed responsibility for the attack.

June 19, 2002
Seven people were killed and thirty-five wounded in an attack at a popular hitch hiking post in East Jerusalem. The al-Aqsa Martyrs' Brigades claimed responsibility for the attack.

July 17, 2002
Four people were killed and twenty-five hospitalized in a dual suicide bombing near Tel Aviv's old station. Of the dead, three were foreign workers in Israel. Islamic Jihad initially claimed responsibility for the attack, although the al-Aqsa Martyrs' Brigades later identified the attackers and also claimed responsibility.

July 30, 2002
At least five people were injured in a suicide attack on a falafel shop in central Jerusalem by Majd 'Atta, a seventeen-year-old from Beit Jala, near Bethlehem. The al-Aqsa Martyrs' Brigades claimed responsibility for the attack.

August 4, 2002
Nine people were killed and thirty-seven injured in a suicide bombing attack on a bus traveling from Haifa to Safed in northern Israel. Of the dead, two were foreign workers in Israel, and three were soldiers. Hamas claimed responsibility for the attack.

APPENDIX TWO: CHARTS

All charts relate to suicide attacks on Israeli civilians carried out from September 30, 2000 to August 31, 2002.

Chart 1
Overview: Suicide Bombings Attacks on Civilians

Chart 2
Timeline: Number of Suicide Bombing Attacks

Chart 4
Timeline: Number of Suicide Attacks Indicating Perpetrator Groups

Chart 5
Victims killed by Suicide Bombers

Chart 7
Proportion of Military to Civilian Victims by Perpetrator Group

Chart 8
Number of Suicide Bombing Attacks, by Four Main Perpetrator Groups

Chart 9
Victims killed in suicide bombing attacks, by Four Main Perpetrator Groups

Chart 10
Hamas: Basic Statistics

Chart 11
The al-Aqsa Martyrs' Brigades: Basic Statistics

Chart 12
PFLP: Basic Statistics

Chart 13
Islamic Jihad: Basic Statistics

CHART 1

Overview: Suicide Bombings Atatcks on Civilians
from September 30, 2000 — August 31, 2002

	Group Responsible						
	Hamas	al –Aqsa	Islamic Jihad	PFLP	Jointly claimed[1]	Not claimed	TOTALS
Number of attacks	22	16	12	3	3	4	60
Attacks in which targets were civilian, indiscriminate and/or disproportionate. [2]	18	12	11	2	2	2	48
Total killed	168	38	31	3	22	0	262
Civilian deaths[3]	153	36	12	3	22	0	226
IDF/police deaths	15	2	19	0	0	0	36
Mean number of victims killed per attack (with standard deviation)	7.63 (8.18)	2.37 (2.98)	2.58 (4.77)	1.00 (1.41)	7.33 (7.91)	N/A	4.57 (6.45)
Total wounded (minimum estimates)	986	435	206	47	185	33	1892
Mean number of victims wounded per attack (with standard deviation)	44.82 (40.48)	27.19 (28.87)	17.17 (14.20)	15.67 (11.44)	61.67 (48.36)	8.25 (12.62)	31.44 (34.97)

[1] There were three attacks for which more than one group claimed responsibility. Islamic Jihad and Hamas issued competing claims of responsibility for the August 9, 2001 attack on the Sbarro pizzeria, Jerusalem, killing fifteen civilians and injuring thirty. Hamas and the PFLP both claimed the May 19, 2002 attack on the Netanya market, killing three civilians and injuring thirty. Islamic Jihad and the Al Aqsa Martyrs' Brigades both claimed the July 17, 2002 attack near Tel Aviv railway station, killing four civilians and injuring twenty-five.

[2] This category does not include eight incidents in which the suicide attack was committed by a bomber during the process of apprehension by the authorities.

[3] Data on the status of victims is based on information from the Israeli Ministry of Foreign Affairs.

CHART 2
Timeline: Number of Suicide Bombing Attacks Against Civilians
September 30, 2000 – August 31, 2002

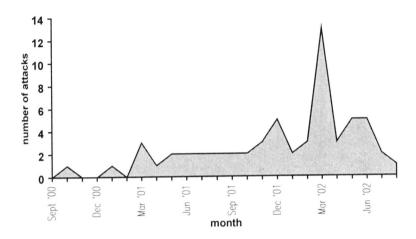

CHART 3
Number of Suicide Attacks Indicating Perpetrator Groups
September 30, 2000 – August 31, 2002

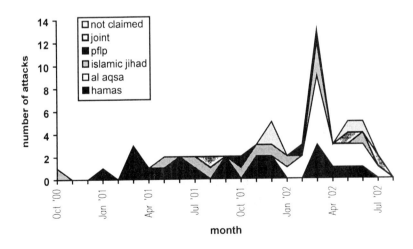

CHART 4

Timeline: Victims Killed by Suicide Bombers from September 30, 2000 – August 31, 2002[1]

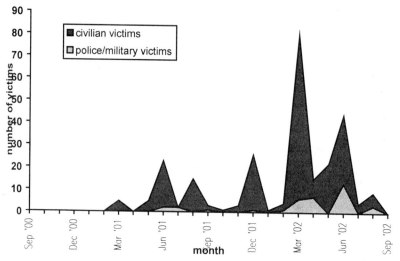

CHART 5

Proportion Of Military To Civilian Victims By Perpetrator Group from September 30, 2000 — August 31, 2002

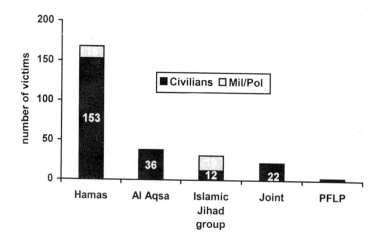

---

[1] Data on the status of victims is based on information from the Israeli Ministry of Foreign Affairs.

CHART 6

Timeline: number of suicide bombing attacks, by four main perpetrator groups from September 30, 2000 — August 31, 2002

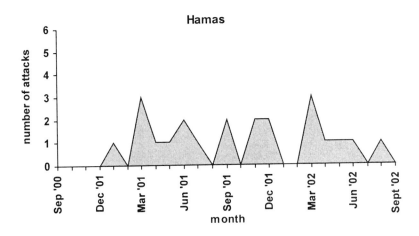

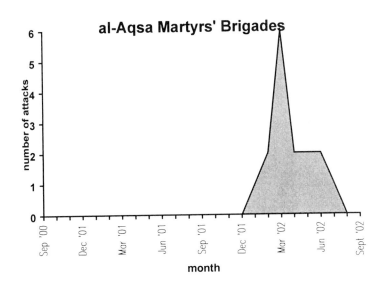

CHART 6 (cont)

Timeline: number of suicide bombing attacks, by four main perpetrator groups from September 30, 2000 — August 31, 2002

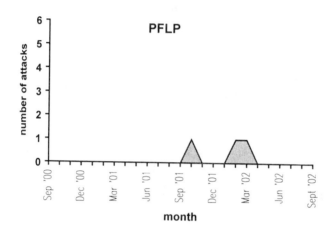

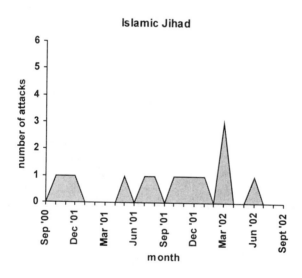

CHART 7

Timeline: victims killed in suicide bombing attacks, by four main perpetrator groups from September 30, 2000 — August 31, 2002

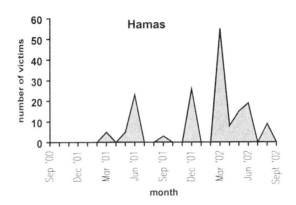

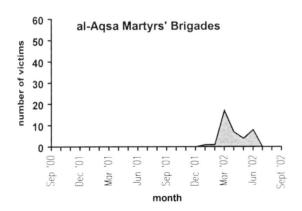

CHART 7 (cont.)

Timeline: victims killed in suicide bombing attacks, by four main perpetrator groups from September 30, 2000 — August 31, 2002

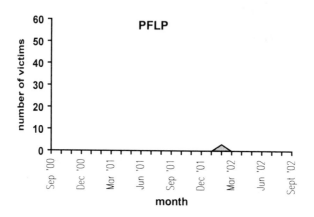

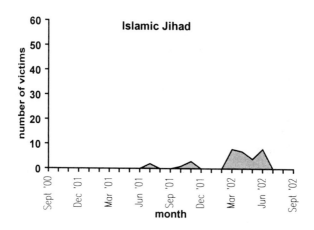

CHART 8

Hamas: Basic Statistics

	Hamas	**Joint[1]**
Number of suicide bombings claimed	22 of 60 total (37%)	2
Attacks in which targets were civilian, indiscriminate, and/or disproportionate	18	
Number of victims killed	168 (64%)	18
Civilian victims killed[2]	153	18
Number of victims wounded (minimum estimates)	986 (52%)	60

Attack Location

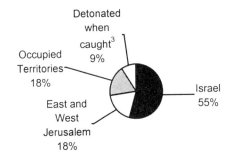

Detonated when caught[3] 9%

Occupied Territories 18%

East and West Jerusalem 18%

Israel 55%

[1] Attacks for which more than one group claimed responsibility. Hamas and Islamic Jihad issued competing claims for responsibility for the August 9, 2001 attack on the Sbarro pizzeria. Hamas and the PFLP issued competing claims for the May 19, 2002 attack on the Netanya market.

[2] Data on the status of victims is based on information from the Israeli Ministry of Foreign Affairs.

[3] This category refers to incidents in which the suicide attack was committed by a bomber during the process of apprehension by the authorities. The intended target of the bomber is thus unknown.

CHART 9

The al-Aqsa Martyrs' Brigades: Basic Statistics

	Al-Aqsa Martyrs' Brigades	Joint[1]
Number claimed	16 of 60 total (27%)	1
Attacks in which targets were civilian, indiscriminate, and/or disproportionate	12	1
Number of victims killed	38 (15%)	4
Civilian victims killed[2]	36	4
Number of victims wounded (minimum estimates)	435 (23%)	25

Attack Location

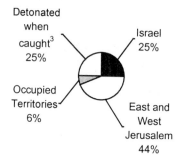

Detonated when caught[3] 25%

Israel 25%

Occupied Territories 6%

East and West Jerusalem 44%

[1] Attacks for which more than one group claimed responsibility. The Al Aqsa Martyrs' Brigades and Islamic Jihad both claimed responsibility for a July 17, 2002 attack near Tel Aviv railway station.

[2] Data on the status of victims is based on information from the Israeli Ministry of Foreign Affairs.

[3] The category refers to incidents in which the suicide attack was committed by a bomber during the process of apprehension by the authorities. The intended target of the bomber is thus unknown.

CHART 10

PFLP: Basic Statistics

	PFLP	**Joint**[1]
Number of suicide bombings claimed	3 of 60 total (5%)	1
Attacks in which targets were civilian, indiscriminate, and/or disproportionate	2	1
Number of victims killed	3 (1%)	3
Civilian victims killed[2]	3	3
Number of victims wounded (minimum estimates)	47 (1%)	30

Attack Location

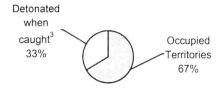

Detonated when caught[3] 33%

Occupied Territories 67%

[1] Attacks for which more than one group claimed responsibility. The PFLP and Hamas issued competing claims for the May 19, 2002 attack on the Netanya market.

[2] Data on the status of victims is based on information from the Israeli Ministry of Foreign Affairs.

[3] This category refers to incidents in which the suicide attack was committed by a bomber during the process of apprehension by the authorities. The intended target of the bomber is thus unknown.

CHART 11

Islamic Jihad: Basic Statistics

	Islamic Jihad	Joint[1]
Number of suicide bombings claimed	12 of 60 total (20%)	2
Attacks in which targets were civilian, indiscriminate, and/or disproportionate	11	2
Number of victims killed	31 (12%)	19
Civilian victims killed[2]	12	19
Number of victims wounded (minimum estimates)	206 (11%)	55

Attack location

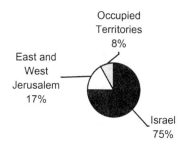

Occupied Territories 8%

East and West Jerusalem 17%

Israel 75%

[1]Attacks for which more than one group claimed responsibility. Islamic Jihad and Hamas issued competing claims of responsibility for the August 9, 2001 attack on the Sbarro pizzeria. The Al Aqsa Martyrs' Brigades and Islamic Jihad both claimed responsibility for a July 17, 2002 attack near Tel Aviv railway station

[2] Data on the status of victims is based on information from the Israeli Ministry of Foreign Affairs.